D1155137

Thomasina Unsworth

After training as an actor, Thomasina worked extensively in both theatre and television. The happy coincidence of pregnancy and a friend asking her to teach a class for them, meant that after ten years as an actor, Thomasina began her teaching career.

She is now Head of First Year at Rose Bruford College. She has been a visiting tutor at various drama schools and universities, teaching and directing. She also works in schools, and as a private acting coach. Thomasina lives in Brighton with her two daughters and husband.

Becoming an Actor

Thomasina Unsworth

NICK HERN BOOKS
London
www.nickhernbooks.co.uk

A NICK HERN BOOK

Becoming an Actor
first published in Great Britain in 2012
by Nick Hern Books Limited,
The Glasshouse, 49a Goldhawk Road, London W12 8QP

Copyright © 2012 Thomasina Unsworth

Thomasina Unsworth has asserted her moral right
to be identified as the author of this work

Cover image © Tumanyan,
used under licence from Shutterstock.com
Cover designed by Nick Hern Books

Typeset by Nick Hern Books
Printed and bound in Great Britain by
T.J. International, Padstow, Cornwall

A CIP catalogue record for this book is available
from the British Library

ISBN 978 1 84842 156 1

MIX
Paper from
responsible sources
FSC® C013056
www.fsc.org

For Isobel and Esme

Contents

Acknowledgements   xi

Introduction   1

Auditioning   5

Part One, First Year
You Are Enough   17
   You Are Enough   18
   Building Blocks   20
   I Want You to Believe Me   23
   Putting It Together   26
Responding Not Instigating   33
   Sharpening Your Senses   34
   Trusting Your Senses   35
   Seeing What is There   37
   Responding to What is There   38
   Basic Repetition   39
   Making It Personal   40
   Noticing the Behaviour   41
   Adding Layers   44
   Another Layer   45
   High Stakes   48
The Significance of Objects   52
   Don't Touch   52
   Endowment   54
Taking Action   57
   Overcoming the Obstacle   58
The Obstacle Within   65
   Pulled in Two Directions   65

Working with Text 72
  Unpacking the Narrative 72
  Changing Chairs 75
  Applying Transitive Verbs 81
  Making Choices 84
  Free Association 87
  Freedom to Play 92
  Breathing the Text 94
Character 97
  Multiple Personalities 97
  Rhythms 100
  Hot-seating 103
  Fifty Questions 104
  Private Moments 108
  The Power of Music 111
Written Work 115
  Writing Your Essay 117

Part Two, the Second Year: Beyond the Self

Beyond the Self 127
Extending Naturalism 129
  The Nature of the Texts 130
  A Different Approach 135
  Making the Text More Concrete 138
  Points of Concentration 141
  Uniting by Subject Change 144
  Clarifying the Subject Changes Further 147
  From One Extreme to Another 148
  Combining the Private with the Public 150
Shakespeare 159
  Problems for the Modern Actor 161
  Making It Your Own 163
  Write Your Own 165
  Finding the Stresses 166

Listening to the Language 169
Exploring without Words 170
Lifting the Line 171
Vowels and Consonants 172
Drawing the Text 174
Landing the Thoughts 175
Marking the Punctuation 176
Taking the Punctuation Away 176
Release 178
Distractions 179
Freedom to Express 179
Rapping 180
Responding 181
The Words Have Been Chosen 182
Staying Alive 183

**Part Three, from Second to Third Year:
Professional Preparation**
Making Contact with the Outside World 191
Headshots 191
Curriculum Vitae 194
Getting an Agent 199
Acting for Camera 209
Radio 212
The Showcase 214
Competitions 219
Independent Research Projects 223
Life Planning 224

Part Four: Life After Drama School
Agents 232
Useful Websites 232
Marketing Yourself 237
Student Films 239

Equity   240
Castings   240
Audition Technique   248
Learning Lines   253
What to Do When You Can't Get Acting Work   256
Surviving Hard Times   262

Appendices
Further Reading   266
Bibliography of Plays   271
Endnotes   272

Acknowledgements

In writing this book I have drawn on the experience and expertise of a number of practitioners; thank you for giving me your valuable time in answering questions and discussing exercises. My colleagues at Rose Bruford College have been a great resource; Iain Reekie, Jeremy Harrison, Julian Jones, Alison MacKinnon, David Zoob, Pat O'Toole, Tess Dignan and Peter Bramley, I have involved you all at some point in this process. Thank you too to Nesta Jones for her support throughout, and to Michael Earley for his help and encouragement. I am very grateful to everyone who contributed to this book, generously offering advice despite hectic workloads: Sooki McShane, Carolyn McLeod, Phillipa Howell, Simon Stephens, Matt Wilde, Paul Whittington, Richard Eyre, Mary FitzGerald, Grant Parsons, Charlotte Jones, Paul Baizley, Colin Hurley, Fiona Dunn and in particular Simon McLindon. I have talked to too many students to name in person, but I am indebted to all of you, not just for your input here, but also for making my job the pleasure that it is.

Many readers will recognise some of the exercises in this book. They are my own distillation of exercises gleaned over the years. Some I have my own drama-school teachers to thank for, others I have discovered further along the line through rehearsals and workshops. Some are adaptations of exercises first put into print by practitioners such as Bella Merlin, Sanford Meisner and Cicely Berry, but may well have been used by actors, teachers and directors before then. I owe a great deal to their inspirational work.

A huge thank-you to Nick Hern and Matt Applewhite.

Introduction

If you are reading this book, there is a good chance that you are thinking of auditioning for drama school. It costs money to attend the rounds of auditions at the top schools and it also takes nerve. You have to stand in front of a panel of people, some of whom may look less than enthusiastic, and convince them of your talent. You will have to show that you have a voice and body that are trainable, that you are responsive and flexible, that you are passionate about what you do, that you are creative and imaginative. You will have to give them a very good reason to select you out of the thousands of applicants auditioning every single year. Each drama school sees well over two thousand hopefuls, and from these they make roughly thirty offers. So behind each person given a place stands a long queue of people wishing that they had been chosen instead. Perhaps if you had only been toying with the idea of trying out for drama school, this paragraph will put you off. If it does then you have had a narrow escape. Auditioning is not for the faint-hearted. You need to want to train as an actor more than anything else in the world in order to endure the experience.

Let us assume that it hasn't deterred you, or perhaps you have already been accepted on to a course. You are, no doubt, aware of what a difficult career you will be preparing for. There are many statistics available showing the awfully small percentage of actors that are in work at any given time; such figures make depressing reading. A large number of those who train face unemployment, others find work for a year or two, perhaps in a soap opera, but then struggle to get another job when their contract has expired. For a fortunate few, long and interesting careers await them. You cannot see into the future, and no one can predict with any certainty how an actor's working life will develop. What you can do is value your training for its own sake and be as prepared as possible for the years beyond it.

Have you any idea what it might actually be like studying at a drama school? When I went to college I felt unprepared, and I wished that I had been better informed. I arrived with lots of preconceptions about what the experience would be and was bewildered initially by how different the reality of the training was in comparison to my fantasy version of it. Had I been better informed, I think I might have got a lot more out of my training. Similarly, when I first went out into the business I was unaware of how much I needed to market myself, or how to deal with various professional situations as they arose. It was tougher than it needed to be.

The aim of this book, then, is not to put you off, because training to be an actor is a wonderful, creative, important thing. The years you spend at a drama school will change you in ways that you could not have foreseen. They will develop your talent, challenge your thinking and nurture your spirit. The years beyond drama school will take you on further adventures. My intention, rather, is to give you a glimpse of what acting classes at an accredited drama school might be like, and to offer you guidance through them and into your first year after graduation. Each school will have its own emphasis and ethos. It's up to you to find out all that you can about each one, before deciding where to apply, or indeed where to attend. I have not taught in every drama school in the land and I am not privy to every eventuality that you might face after you have trained. However, having researched and met with practitioners and industry professionals, I am confident that this book will give you a fair sense of the sorts of exercises that you will come across and the challenges you might face on your journey to becoming an actor.

I have divided the book into four parts covering the three years you will spend at drama school, and the first year after you have left it. The first two sections focus on exercises that you are likely to come across during acting classes. These are not exhaustive, but they will give you a valuable insight into a major element of your training. Of course, you will have all sorts of other classes – chorus and clown, voice, movement, mask, tumbling, stage combat, to name a few – but by focusing on acting I hope you will gain a sense of the spirit behind your training. The third section aims to help you get ready for the profession you have chosen, and covers some practicalities and ideas that you will need to be aware of. The final part offers you guidance through your first year as a professional actor. The first half of the book presents you with lots of exercises and the aims and ideas behind them, the second attempts to answer a series of questions that students often ask.

Never stop asking yourself if acting really is what you want to do with your life. If you continue to answer 'Yes' to that question, then ask yourself what you need to do so that becoming an actor becomes a reality. I hope that this book will help you on your way.

Auditioning

In order to gain a place at a drama school, you need to be a talented actor; however, sometimes even that is not enough. Gifted actors often do not do themselves justice when they come to audition. With this in mind, the aims of this chapter are:

- To prepare you for some of the discrepancies that you might come across when you audition at different drama schools.

- To give you an insight into the sort of qualities that the people auditioning you will be looking for.

- To show you some broad examples of poor auditions.

- To highlight some of the potential pitfalls.

Auditions will vary from school to school in terms of the way that they are structured, so do not expect the same process each time. At some schools you will be expected to do your audition speeches in front of the other candidates, and there could be as many as forty other people in the room with you. This means that not only will you have to perform in front of a sizeable audience, but that you will also have to sit and listen to all those other speeches. It is easy to lose your energy in this situation. It is also easy to be influenced by other versions of your speech that you might hear. You need to keep focused on what you are doing and to remember the reasons behind the choices that you have already made.

Make sure that you read all the information that is sent to you by each of the drama schools regarding their audition requirements, as these will not all be the same. For example:

- Some schools ask for three speeches, two classical and one modern.

- Some will specify the date after which your modern play must have been written.

- Some blacklist certain speeches and writers.

- Some request that you do not use monologues from film scripts, your own writing, or the work of little-known authors.

Do not assume that you can just learn two speeches and that these will serve you for every audition that you attend.

The time that you spend in the audition room will also vary from place to place. At some schools the first round of auditioning is a speedy event: you may well feel that you have hardly walked into the room before it is time to leave it. Do not read anything into the length of time that you spend in front of the panel, as the people auditioning you may know very quickly whether or not they want to call you back. On some occasions you will be asked questions during the first round, or be asked to try the piece again in a different way. At the recall stage, the panel will certainly want to talk to you after you have done your speeches.

The size of the panel of people auditioning you will also differ from school to school. You might find yourself in front of just one person, or you could be faced by a row of four or more people. It is unlikely, however, that at recall stages you would meet only one person – the recall panel tends to be made up of a number of people covering different disciplines, such as voice and movement, as well as acting.

For some auditions you will be asked to prepare a song. Remember, unless you are applying for a musical-theatre course, the quality of your singing voice is not the main concern. What will interest an audition panel is how well you communicate the story of the song. The challenge, therefore, is an acting one, so don't panic if singing is not your strong point. Make sure that you are well prepared and that you have a strong connection to the lyrics.

During some auditions you will be asked to work with other people: be open to this and responsive to what someone else might be offering you. You may do your speech very well, but if you cannot work with another human being, you will certainly not be offered a place to train as an actor. You may find that there are several rounds of auditions to get through before you are accepted, and it is highly likely that at the later stages of the process you will be required to work with other actors.

The feel of each drama school that you apply to will be quite different. Before you arrive at an audition, take the time to read the prospectus or look at what the college says about itself on its website. When you arrive, talk to students already studying there. Walk about and ask questions; think about whether you can visualise yourself there. It may be that you are offered a place at more than one school, and you need to be equipped to make the right choice. Even if you are only offered a place at one institution, you don't want to accept if you think that the next three years will be miserable!

Although drama schools may vary in the way that they audition candidates, they will almost certainly be looking for similar qualities in those that they offer places to. Obviously raw talent is the key factor that a panel will look for, but a successful applicant will also:

- Have a connection to their speeches and will have contextualised them within the plays that they belong to.

- Be imaginative.

- Be flexible and open to redirection.

- Be passionate and serious about acting.

- Have an opinion about film, television and theatre.

- Have bodies and voices that are not so locked and stiff that they cannot be trained.

- Work responsively with others.

- Be well prepared.

- Be playful and bold.

Here are four fictional – but surprisingly accurate – excerpts from typical auditions to help you spot the candidates that don't adhere to the list above!

Richard

PANELLIST. Your speeches were really good but I just want to play around with them a bit.

RICHARD. Okay. (*Rests his hands on the back of the chair he has been using.*)

PANELLIST. Well, for a start, let's get rid of that chair. Let's clear it to the side of the room.

RICHARD. What, I can't use the chair?

PANELLIST. Let's try it without.

RICHARD. But I have rehearsed with it.

PANELLIST. That's okay, something different will happen. Also, we know that the character is alone during this speech, but can you imagine that he is actually in public? Let's say he is standing in the middle of a very crowded bus. He needs to voice his thoughts, but he doesn't want anyone else to hear him.

RICHARD. But that won't work: it isn't written like that!

Louise

PANELLIST. Those speeches were very interesting and you responded well to what we asked you to do with them. Come and sit down and tell me, why do you want to be an actor?

LOUISE (*looking surprised*). Well, everyone said I should.

PANELLIST. And what do you think?

LOUISE. Yeah, I think it would be good.

PANELLIST. What theatre have you seen, good or bad?

LOUISE. I can't think right now.

PANELLIST. What about films?

LOUISE. I quite like Johnny Depp. He's good.

PANELLIST. In what way 'good'? What does he do?

LOUISE. Oh... I don't know, he's just good, isn't he?

William

WILLIAM (*poking his head around the door*). Sorry, it's just that I am meeting a friend. I didn't realise that the auditions would take this long. Shall I come back another day?

PANELLIST. No.

Tracy

TRACY. I have been really busy with work recently and I haven't learnt this as well as I wanted to, so if I go wrong, it's just because of that.

PANELLIST....?

These are very obvious examples of people not doing themselves justice in an audition situation, and I am sure that you would not behave like any of them – however, there are things that you do need to be aware of:

Choose your speeches carefully – find ones that not only contrast with each other, but also that you enjoy, have a connection with and can relate to. Make sure that you have read the whole play and can contextualise the speech. Almost every school will want you to prepare a piece from a classical play (e.g. Shakespeare) and a piece from a modern play (e.g. Simon Stephens). It is likely that you will be asked to concentrate more on your classical speech than your modern during the audition, but prepare both equally. It is worth having a couple of 'spare' speeches up your sleeve in case the auditioning panel wants to see something different. Think about the impact that your speech will have on those listening to it: angry rants about infanticide or sexual deviancy can be difficult to listen to, particularly if not done well. If you have chosen something that requires very heightened emotions, make sure that you can really connect with it. Sometimes when people get nervous they find it difficult to access their emotional resources in the way that they did in rehearsal, and there is nothing worse than watching someone push for feelings that they are not even close to experiencing. If tears don't come, don't pretend that they have: you don't get extra points for crying anyway, so make different choices and don't strive to fake it. If you don't think that you will be able to do this, then avoid choosing texts that require extremes of emotion.

Prepare well so if nerves come and temporarily wipe your mind clear of your lines, you will be so familiar with the text that you will be able to get back on track easily. If you do forget the words, pause and keep breathing. If you are near the beginning, you could ask to start again. Otherwise remember the story that you are telling and allow the lines to come back to you. Everyone appreciates that you will be nervous, and the people auditioning you should be fairly understanding, so don't panic. Think about *what* you are communicating rather than *how* you are communicating it, and if the lines are securely there in the first place you should get them back. It is a horrible experience to go blank during an audition, but if you are very well prepared you will feel more confident and so less likely to forget your lines in the first place – and more able to move on if you do.

Resist making excuses for things not going well. Unless you are specifically asked if there is a problem, don't bring up issues such as tiredness or illness that might prevent you doing your best. You have to do your best regardless of how much sleep you have had or how swollen your tonsils are. If you start making excuses it sounds as if you are trying to hide the fact that you aren't very good. The people auditioning you will be able to see if you aren't entirely well and will be sympathetic; you don't need to highlight problems before you start or apologise after you have finished – if you are really ill, you shouldn't be at the audition. If you are at the audition, then you have to get on with it; it is amazing how adrenalin will get you through on the day.

Think where you should place yourself in relation to the audition panel. You shouldn't stand too close, as this can be intimidating for all concerned. Some people won't mind being looked at directly, some will, but you could ask before you start if you are anxious about it. Remember, if you do make eye contact with the people auditioning you, then be prepared to see them taking notes and consulting with each other. Don't let this put you off.

Take your time before you start. Give yourself a chance to think about what you are doing. Don't rush the speech. You may only have a few moments to impress so don't waste them.

Go with redirection – you may well be asked to try the speech from a different angle, even if it seems to make no sense within the context of the play as a whole. Be bold and playful and open to suggestions. The panel will simply be trying to find out how responsive and imaginative you are.

In conversation, have an idea about the sort of acting you like. You won't be expected to have seen everything, but you need to have an opinion about the things that you have seen. It doesn't matter whether you talk about a school play or a piece of new writing at the Royal Court Theatre, it is your interest in it that you need to communicate, your passion. Before the audition you should think about the sort of questions that you might be asked so that you can do yourself justice with the answers. Think about what your response might be if you were asked why you want to go to that particular college? Whose career you aspire to? What is unique about you? Where you see yourself in ten years' time? You cannot anticipate every question that you might be asked, but you can guess at the sort of things a panel might like to know about you. There is no right or wrong response to a question, so do not strive to be impressive or to curry favour with the questioner. Try to answer honestly and thoughtfully.

Resist drawing unnecessary attention to yourself – wear neutral clothes that you feel good in and that you can move easily in. Don't wear too much make-up!

Remember, many people aren't successful in their first attempt to get into a drama school. It may be that the people auditioning you will think you are not ready yet. They may have already offered an actor very like you a place, and they may be looking for someone different so that the group is balanced. Sometimes people auditioning you make a mistake. All in all, it is a really tough process: you need to distance yourself a little from it so that you can be objective about how it went, and decide what to do if you don't get in. These auditions cost money and you will probably be doing a few of them. They also cost you personally and can be nerve-racking. You need to be in control of the experience and recognise if and when you are wasting your time, and your money, by persisting.

Part One
First Year

You Are Enough

When you first arrive at drama school you may well feel the need to establish yourself within the group. It is natural that you will want to justify your place on the course to the other students and the teachers. You may feel competitive and want to demonstrate that you are the best actor that ever walked through the door. Or you may be ambushed by self-doubt and seek to compensate for this by proving that you are actually really really good. You might even feel paralysed by the whole experience.

Early classes are designed with all this in mind. The desire to impress or the onslaught of fear will only succeed in blocking you as an actor. They are barriers that prevent you from being 'open'. If you are not open then how can you respond honestly to another human being or to a piece of text? How can you communicate a story so that it reaches an audience and affects them? No matter how skilled you are, *you* will always get in the way. The purpose of the following section is not to teach you to act; I would argue that no one can really do that. Instead, these exercises should work on the things that block you, they should chip away at whatever it is that prevents you from being the best actor that you are capable of being.

Aims

- To introduce you to key questions, such as what is theatre? What is acting? What is performance?

- To encourage you to think about your own behaviour and that of those you are watching.

- To introduce you to some useful vocabulary.

- To introduce you to the concept of being 'private' in public.

- To begin to tackle the issue of self-consciousness for you as an actor.

- To encourage you to think about *what* you are doing rather than *how* you are doing it.

- To encourage you to watch other people work closely, and to analyse what you see in relation to your own practice.

You Are Enough

Divide the space into two sections, marking them out clearly with a line.

Stand with the rest of the actors on one side of this line. This then becomes the 'offstage space'. Across the divide is the 'onstage space'.

You will be called one by one to enter the onstage space. Those remaining behind the line keep observing.

There is only one rule that you must remember when you cross the line and that is: *if you think of something interesting to do, don't do it!* In other words, don't plan what you are going to do in the space. Don't think of funny or engaging ways to entertain the audience. Resist the temptation to perform, just allow things to happen in that moment. For example, if you feel like lying down, lie down, if you want to look at the wall, look at it, if your head is itching, scratch it. There is no need to make any eye contact with those watching, or to acknowledge them at all.

This is a non-verbal exercise. If relationships occur between those in the onstage space, then these must not be expressed through words. For example, you may want to touch someone, or sit with them, or even walk away from them. Respond to each other in any way that feels appropriate, but not through speech.

After some time, objects will be handed to the actors in the onstage space. For example, you might be given a tape measure, a pack of cards or a bouncy ball. Do what you want with these objects but remember the rule: *if you think of something interesting to do, don't do it!* In other words, use the object in any way that you want to, but do so without considering the effect that your actions will have on the audience.

Eventually, everyone will be in the onstage space, except one person who is still observing. When you are given the instruction, those being observed will turn to watch this remaining individual. So the observer becomes the observed, and vice versa.

This work comes from classes developed by theatre practitioner Julian Jones. It encourages you to look at what it is to be in the audience and what it is to be in front of the audience. Traditionally, this is how theatre works: one group of people watches another. The instruction – 'if you think of something interesting to do, don't do it!' – goes to the heart of the exercise. As soon as you stop being the observer and cross the line into the territory of the observed, something will change in you. Almost certainly you will become self-conscious, no longer relaxed but now acutely aware of being watched. As a result, you may well begin to project an image of yourself onto the audience. You may want to appear at ease, to be entertaining. How does the actor eradicate feelings of self-consciousness, and the accompanying compulsions to cover them by performing in some way? This exercise offers you a starting point from which to address this question – you can build from it.

Remember, what is interesting about you is what is unique about you, your breath, your heartbeat, your complexities. It is far less compelling to watch you doing an impression of yourself, or anyone else for that matter. Mimicry gets quite dull after a while. In essence, you are enough, and when you engage with this idea and let go of the desire to perform, something really exciting can happen.

When you are given the object, use it if you want to, don't pretend to do so. Don't fake playing cards or measure the room in a comedic manner. When you come into contact with a fellow human being, don't try to make an interesting picture together, see what actually happens between you without you trying to force anything.

Building Blocks

a. The group is split into two: half of you go outside and wait while the other half stays in the room.

Those in the room hide a set of keys.

When the hiding place has been established, those of you waiting outside will enter the room, one by one, and look for the keys. Those inside observe the searchers.

When everyone has had a turn the two groups swap over and the observed become the observers.

At the end of the exercise you should talk both about what it felt like and also what you noticed from watching the others search for the keys.

b. Repeat this exercise in the same way, with half the group watching and half the group doing. This time, those going out of the room are shown where the keys will be hidden.

One by one, re-enter the room to look for the keys as you did in the previous exercise.

After everyone has had a turn, compare the two experiences – one when you didn't know where the keys were, and the second one when you did. Think about it both in terms of your experience doing the exercises yourself, and then watching others do them.

c. The group is divided into two as before. Half leave the room, the other half find a hiding place for the keys.

Some of those waiting outside, but not all, are told where the keys have been hidden.

One by one, enter the room and search for the keys. Those watching have to decide who is genuinely looking for the keys and who is pretending to do so.

You might be provided with extra information as you search. For example, you might be told that you are looking for the keys to a cupboard, which a small child has locked himself into. The stakes might be raised even higher: for instance, you might then be told that this child, who is now becoming frightened, suffers from severe asthma triggered by stress!

When everyone has had a chance to look for the keys, the groups then swap over, so that the observers become the observed, and vice versa. After you have all had a turn in both roles you should then discuss with each other who you think knew the whereabouts of the keys and who didn't. Make it clear why you arrive at your conclusions.

You can see that these exercises slowly build on each other. Previously, you were asked to be in a space in front of other people and to observe what happened. Here you were asked to be in a space in front of other people, but you were also asked to find some keys that had been hidden. You were given a reason for entering the space. You probably found it much easier to be watched when you had a purpose to focus on. Having a purpose gives you something to hold on to, it gives you a direction to follow. You need a reason to enter the onstage space.

That was easy enough, but perhaps you found that it got difficult again when you had to pretend that you didn't know where the keys were. Often people work very hard to indicate that they are not, in fact, pretending. I have seen actors spend a disproportionate length of time jumping up to try and reach a ledge that is so far out of anybody's reach that the keys could not be hidden there. I have seen others empty bags with grand flourishes, pulling items out in a great rush without noticing what they are discarding. The keys might very well be there, but they have no real interest in finding them. Their focus is instead on showing the audience that they don't know the hiding place, rather than on seeing whether the keys are in the bag. I have even seen someone put their hand on the keys and then pull it hurriedly away and walk off, assuming that this would fool the audience into thinking that they didn't know that they were there! These actors are very busy *showing* us that they are looking for the keys, and so they reveal that their purpose is to deceive the audience. They have disconnected from the actual purpose that would make an audience believe them, and that is to find the keys.

The people who are genuinely ignorant of the hiding place tend to really look for the keys! Their focus is on this objective because they have nothing else to worry about. When they look through a bag, they really look. When this sense of purpose is intensified with extra information, then the actor's focus becomes sharpened further. If you engage your imagination and think why you need that key, what it unlocks, what would happen if you failed to find it, etc., then once again you will be thinking of the task itself and not of how you are coming across to the people watching you. A sense of purpose and an imaginative connection to the situation will really help you here.

I Want You to Believe Me

In groups of three, exchange stories about your lives that are significant to you. These should not be too lengthy and they should have a clear narrative structure. In other words: a beginning, a middle, and an end.

Here is an example to give you an idea of what I mean – your story will come from your own life but it will follow a similar narrative structure: I might choose to tell the story of when I was ten years old and stole a bar of chocolate from my local newsagent's. I *begin* by detailing how I felt before I entered the shop. How it took a while for me to pluck up the courage to open the door. My *middle* section deals with the theft itself. I describe how the shop looked inside. How I loitered by the shelf with all the chocolates on it. How I watched the shopkeeper before grabbing the bar and stuffing it into my pocket. How I tried to look nonchalant and stroll out of the shop even when I wanted to make a run for it. My *final* section describes how guilty I felt afterwards, and how when I got the bar out of my pocket I had lost my appetite for it, because all I could think of was what my dad would say if he knew I had stolen something. I relate how in the distance I heard the wail of a police siren, which seemed to grow louder and louder, causing me to reason that the police must be closing in on me having discovered my crime. I describe how, in a panic, I threw the chocolate bar into someone's front garden and ran all the way home in tears.

In your group of three, choose one of the stories, which you must then all adopt as your own. This means two of the three will have to adapt the facts to make the story more specific to them. For example, if the story chosen is about a Scottish woman and you are a Welshman, you must change the details so that the story fits you just as well.

Having maintained the overall sense and trajectory of the story, keeping it as close to the original as possible whilst endowing it with facts pertinent to you, each of you must now tell the story out loud.

The rest of the class listens to each story and then decides through discussion who the story actually originated with.

Following on from the exercise with the keys, the aim of this exercise is to challenge your perception of what you need to do in order to make people believe you. Be careful: it is very tempting to show how forcefully you are feeling when you tell the story, thinking that this will make you more credible. You might try to connect to some sadness within it and so push for tears. You might add pauses to build suspense, or you might try to hesitate and stumble as you speak to show that the memories are coming to you there and then. But if you do any of this, we will know that you are faking! Think about the story itself, not how you are delivering it; about what you are saying and not how you are saying it. In other words, don't think about you! Ask yourself: does a story become more credible the more someone shows us how they are feeling? We will get on to story-telling later, but it is worth giving this some thought now. Have you noticed that often when someone is talking about something unsettling that has happened to them, they will try to put a lid on their emotions? These emotions tend to seep out anyway in a myriad of different ways, but the aim of the teller is not to be emotional but to communicate the story. Interestingly, it is not necessarily the person whose story it actually is who always appears the most convincing. Sometimes this person tries to make their story sound more interesting or dynamic once they get in front of an audience, and this detracts from their credibility.

Putting It Together

Before the session starts, think of something simple that you might need to do. If it isn't something that is immediately pressing, think of a time when it was or imagine a time when it will be.

Here are some examples:

- I need to decorate a cake for my best friend's birthday.

- I need to tidy my room.

- I need to prepare for a party I am having.

- I need to get ready for college tomorrow.

This is your *objective*. In order to explain the exercise, let's take 'I need to get ready for college tomorrow' as an example.

Having thought of the objective, you should then ask yourself a further question: 'Why do I need to do this? In order for what to happen?' Here is how you might answer this question:

- I need to get ready for college tomorrow in order to train as an actor so that I can impress my parents who never thought that I would amount to much.

Call this deeper wish the *super-objective*.

Objective:
I need to get ready for college tomorrow.

Super-objective:
To impress my faithless parents.

In exploring the deeper wish, really probe so that you can begin to get a clear sense of what the broader need sheltering the immediate objective might be.

Now you have an objective and a super-objective, carry on asking yourself questions. The questions here apply to your *given circumstances*, which inform your behaviour and the choices that you make. For example, you will behave differently if it is late at night, or first thing in the morning; you have just been with your lover, or your mother; it is snowing outside, or the sun is burning through the window.

- Where am I? (*Your physical surroundings.*)

- When is it? (*Time, day, season.*)

- What have I just been doing?

- Why do I need this now?

- What will happen if I don't achieve my objective?

- What might stop me achieving my objective?

- What am I going to do in order to achieve my objective?

In answer to 'What am I going to do in order to achieve my objective?', think of three physical actions that you might engage in. For example:

Objective:
I need to get ready for college tomorrow.

Physical actions:
I pack a bag.
I iron a shirt.
I prepare a sandwich for lunch.

Each activity you choose should last about five minutes. They can overlap. They must be active; you cannot choose to lie down and sleep or to read a book in a corner! All the physical actions take place in real time, so if you are ironing a shirt, you will need to heat the iron so that it is hot enough to accomplish the task. You should not have music on whilst you do the exercise. You should not use words. You should rehearse the physical actions at home and relate them to the questions listed above in preparation.

Furniture will be provided for you, so there is no need to bring in beds and chests of drawers, etc.! However, as there can be no miming, you will need to bring all the props required for your activities. You should also bring in things that will help you recreate the space that you rehearsed in. If this is your bedroom then bring in your own duvet, photographs, candles, etc. Bring in anything that will help to stimulate your imagination.

Having set up your space, carry out the physical actions you have rehearsed. Afterwards you should talk about your experience and hear what those watching you noticed.

This work is grounded in the ideas and practices of Konstantin Stanislavsky. In this instance, the exercise is being used to continue the work on what happens to us when we are observed. Bearing this in mind, do not be tempted to be original or even interesting when you are preparing. Choose an objective that you can relate to – it doesn't matter how mundane it might seem. If you choose something that you have absolutely no experience of, or feelings for, you will really struggle here. The aim is never to impress, but the exercise goes some way towards addressing the feelings of self-consciousness that you might experience when being observed. If you concentrate on what you are doing, on the physical actions that you have chosen, you will not be thinking about how you are coming across to the audience. You will be released from that awful burden of having to be entertaining!

Interesting things can happen when you work like this. I have seen actors discover a whole raft of emotions just through getting on with their tasks. For example, an actor who started his exercise by methodically sorting photographs to put in an album became paralysed by feelings of homesickness. He was so affected that he could not put one particular picture down and sat arrested by a sense of loss, clutching the photo quite besieged by his grief. The physical action came first – he had focused on putting the photographs into the album, he had not begun by trying to generate great emotion. If you start by trying to generate emotion then all you are doing is thinking of yourself and how you are coming across, you are not thinking of your task. Don't think about yourself!

During exercises some people may have a profound experience, such as the one outlined above, others won't. Never compare yourself to others, that's a miserable path to go down and it can paralyse you. Find what is useful to you in the exercise, whatever your experience of it is – and remember that you learn from watching as well as doing.

Prepare well. Relate what you are doing to the list of questions. Do think in terms of needs not wants – you might *want* a piece of cake but you can do with out it. *Needing* something is harder to ignore, and so is much more valuable to you as an actor. You may have noticed that I did not ask you to answer the question 'Who am I?' when you were thinking about all the given circumstances. That is because this question is a limited one as it supposes that there is only one answer to it and that you are a fixed entity. Of course you are not a fixed and unchanging thing; you adapt constantly to your environment and to the circumstances you find yourself in. The director Declan Donnellan[1] very usefully suggests that it would be more helpful to ask the questions 'Who would I like to be?' and 'Who am I afraid I might be?' You could try this out when you are preparing.

It is helpful when you do this exercise to think about everything that you are doing as being in response to something else that has gone before. For example, if you pack your movement kit into your bag it is because your timetable says that you have movement the next day; you iron a shirt because you want to make a good impression on a girl that you noticed during induction week; you prepare a sandwich because you realise you haven't enough money left to buy anything from the canteen. All the little moments are a series of responses too. Think about what informs your everyday thoughts and actions. Nothing comes from nothing.

You should also be responsive during the exercise to all the unexpected things that happen. If someone shouts outside the window or it starts to pour with rain so loudly that the water drums down onto the roof, don't pretend it isn't happening just because it didn't during your rehearsals – what you rehearsed is only a part of this process. It is a fundamental requirement of a good actor that they are able to respond to what is happening in that moment. An actor once told me that she thought that if she kept things small then she would come across as being more honest. As a result, during this exercise she focused only on what was happening right in front of her. When the door to the next classroom slammed really loudly and unexpectedly, she pretended not to hear it because by doing so she would have to operate within a wider radius, and anyway it hadn't happened in rehearsals. It was safer to keep her focus concentrated within the tiny circle that she had created for herself, but by doing so she wasn't alive to what was around her: she was being utterly self-conscious and actually utterly dishonest.

I have referred you to some key terms here such as *objective*, *super-objective* and *given circumstances.* Never get hung up with the jargon. Different people will use these terms slightly differently. It doesn't matter what you call things as long as you understand what it is you are trying to explore in a particular exercise.

These exercises are fluid and can be used in a variety of contexts, providing you with a raft of things to think about. Through them, however, you should have been:

- Challenged to think about the differences you experience between being the observed and being the observer, and about how each of these roles alters your behaviour.

- Encouraged to understand that you are interesting, but that a representation of a self that you think will be entertaining or impressive, isn't.

- Shown the importance of having a purpose when you come into the 'onstage space'.

- Pushed to focus on the thing that you are doing, not on how the audience is responding to you doing it.

- Introduced to some useful terminology and questions that, if you engage with them, should affect your behaviour.

- Given the opportunity to experience bringing something that you did privately into a public arena and noting the difference.

- Discouraged from trying to generate emotion artificially, and instead urged to explore the possibility that emotions can arise out of what you are doing.

- Encouraged to respond to what is going on around you and inside yourself in that moment, even if it was not something that you had prepared for.

Responding
Not Instigating

Like all animals, human beings are responsive creatures. Our behaviour is governed by a multitude of stimuli. We may run when we are chased; we may cry when we remember something sad; we may become aroused when we meet someone attractive; we may put on a jumper when we are cold. These are tangible, specific things, to which we react in one way or another. It is very important that you remember this and do not feel that, when you are acting, you need to dredge up emotions from a general heap of feelings located somewhere inside of you. You do not need to commit to actions that bear no relation to what you are actually experiencing in that moment. The purpose of the following exercises is to really encourage you to resist the solipsistic, emotive acting that one so often sees, and to begin to work responsively and so more honestly.

Aims

- To discourage you from looking inwards for answers.

- To ask you to work with all your senses engaged.

- To ask you to work without censorship.

- To discourage you from anticipating the next moment.

- To show you the importance of paying limitless amounts of attention to those you are working with.

- To encourage you to be active as a result of what someone else does to you.

Sharpening Your Senses

Form a wide circle, which will mark out the playing area. Those forming it should act as a barrier so that people inside it will not leave it and harm themselves. Remember to be as quiet as possible while the game is being played.

Two of you enter the circle and stand apart from each other. You will each be given a rolled-up newspaper. You will then be blindfolded and turned around to disorientate you.

A set of keys will be placed on the floor in front of one of you. You will be allowed to touch them so that you have located them but you will not be allowed to cover them with your hand or body for any length of time. You are the guard of the castle and your objective is to prevent anyone from stealing those keys.

The other one of you does not know where the keys are, but your objective is to locate and steal them. You are the robber.

While the rest of the group watches, you both play your objectives. Do not become violent with the newspaper!

This exercise encourages you to rely on senses other than your sight. We place a lot of importance on seeing someone or something, but when we can no longer do this we have to work harder to listen, smell and touch. If all of your senses are alert, then you will have so much more stimuli to respond to. You really will be alive to what is going on around you, and this will be reflected in your body, making you more dynamic.

Be careful not to panic during this exercise and start swiping randomly at the air. Listen, feel, sense. Use strategies to gain your objective, don't just rush at the game like an animal being attacked. Focus on where the other person might be and on all the sounds that might betray them. Do not place your attention on yourself but on your opponent. Take your time.

Trusting Your Senses

One person is chosen to stand in front of the others, who line up across the other side of the room. If it is you, hold your hand outstretched in front of you.

One by one, each of the group crosses the room and rests their hand against yours. Observe closely how they move and make sure you get a really good sense of each person before you release them from the contact.

Having done this, repeat the process – but this time you are blindfolded or have your eyes closed as each member of the group comes up to touch your hand. The order in which people cross the room should be changed at each stage of this exercise.

As each person touches your hand, say the name of the person you think it is out loud without removing the blindfold or opening your eyes. You will not be told whether you are right or wrong. Continue until everyone has made contact with you again, then open your eyes and see how many people you named correctly.

Repeat the process, but this time no one will actually touch your hand. They will leave a centimetre or so between their palm and yours. Keep your eyes shut or blindfolded until the end and then see how many people you managed to name correctly.

Those of you crossing the room, make sure that you do not start walking until the last person has left the space and is still. This allows the person sensing who you are to really listen to you approaching and not confuse your rhythms with someone else's.

The exercise continues until everyone has filled the solo spot.

This is an exercise that should be repeated regularly as you become more responsive to each other. Notice how people give away their identity even when you cannot see or touch them: the rhythm of their walk, the length of their stride, whether they lift their feet off the ground or not, their smell, the shadow they cast as they stand in front of you, the heat that comes from them, are all clues. Don't strive to get it right, allow your instincts to work. As with all the other exercises, this is not a test that must be passed, it is an exploration to see what happens when you engage your senses and open up to each other.

Seeing What is There

Divide into pairs. One of you is A, the other B. Sit facing each other.

As A, you tell your partner what you see when you look at them.

For example:

'You have blue eyes.'

'You have long eyelashes.'

'You have dark shadows under your eyes.'

'Your nose slopes to the right.'

This communication happens without comment or judgement from either of you.

When you have remarked on everything that you can see, look again and see some more. Keep looking in more and more detail. Do not swap over until you have examined every inch of your partner's face. Then it is B's turn.

Do not try to be polite during this exercise and censor statements that you think might cause offence. If someone has a spot, they have a spot; if their mouth turns down, it turns down. You are not passing judgement or being judged. One of you is simply saying what they see at that moment, and the other is allowing you to do so. Notice how much more there is to see in someone when you really start looking. It is easy to clock someone's basic features, but all the textures, colours, angles of a face will be missed if you regard it only superficially.

Responding to What is There

Stand facing your partner on a diagonal. The rest of the group watch. Resist the pressure you may feel as a result of being observed to do anything interesting. Simply maintain eye contact and take in everything that is going on with the other person.

If you have an impulse to respond in any way as a result of how your partner's behaviour affects you, then do so without censorship or comment. You may touch your partner if you feel the need to.

This is a non-verbal exercise.

Plenty of time should be allocated to it.

In order to clarify this exercise, let me give you a rather memorable example of it in action. At the beginning of the exercise, the two actors stood facing each other across the room. Nothing happened and the silence between them seemed solid. As the moments passed, the atmosphere became increasingly charged. Actor A began to actively scrutinise his partner, seeking to observe something that would galvanise him into action. Actor B seemed to be doing nothing in response to this, so eventually actor A gave up and both actors began to relax. Their breathing became less shallow, they became more absorbed in each other and gradually they began to communicate. As he saw his partner visibly relax, actor A smiled, and in response actor B raised an eyebrow. They twitched their big toes simultaneously and that made both of them laugh. Those watching observed a sort of dance begin, slow and tentative, with actor A being more assertive than his partner. After some time, actor A leant in to kiss his partner on the lips. Immediately his partner recoiled in obvious disgust. Actor A was clearly embarrassed and left the room. Actor B watched him go, not knowing whether to stay and so avoid him or to follow and comfort him.

Nothing as dramatic as this might happen when you do the exercise. Don't compare yourself to others; your own experiences may well not mirror theirs. Respond openly to what your partner does to you and how that makes you feel. Dare to do nothing if you have no impulse to do anything else. Conversely, dare to go with your impulses and do not check them. Be attentive only to what is happening in that moment with your partner; do not attempt to anticipate the next or link to the one that went before. It is not your responsibility to construct a narrative, those watching can do that for themselves if one suggests itself.

Basic Repetition

In pairs, label yourselves A and B.

A makes a simple observation about B. For example: 'You are wearing a black shirt.'

This statement is repeated between them until they are asked to swap over, and then it is B's turn to make an observation about A. For example:

A. You are wearing a black shirt.

B. You are wearing a black shirt.

A. You are wearing a black shirt.

B. You are wearing a black shirt.

A. You are wearing a black shirt.

B. You have blue eyes.

A. You have blue eyes.

B. You have blue eyes.

A. You have blue eyes.

This exercise derives from the work of Sanford Meisner, as do the rest of the exercises that follow in this section. It is very, very basic, but often actors struggle initially to accept its simplicity. You may want to colour the words or add inflections to make the sentence seem more dynamic, but you must resist the urge. Make sure you listen to each other. It is very easy to come in with your part of the repetition before your partner has finished theirs. All you have to do is listen and repeat what you hear. You are not mimicking an accent, you are repeating the words that your partner speaks.

Making It Personal

Do exactly as you did in the previous exercise, but this time repeat the observation from your own point of view. For example:

A. You have brown hair.

B. I have brown hair.

A. You have brown hair.

B. I have brown hair.

When you are told to, swap over so that B makes the initial observation. For example:

B. You have a mole on your cheek.

A. I have a mole on my cheek.

B. You have a mole on your cheek.

A. I have a mole on my cheek.

Although communication between people was happening during the previous exercise, here you are moving towards something that should feel more human and less robotic. You are listening and repeating without comment or embellishment, but this time you are also responding from your own point of view, which will feel more natural.

Noticing the Behaviour

Continue with the previous exercise, repeating from you own point of view, but this time as well as their physical attributes, take a look at your partner's behaviour. Whenever you see a change in that behaviour, voice it. You can do this whether you are A or B, you don't have to wait your turn to notice the behaviour change as it occurs in your partner. Here is an example of the sort of thing that I mean:

A. You have brown hair.

B. I have brown hair.

A. You have brown hair.

B. You are smiling.

A. I am smiling.

B. You are laughing.

A. I am laughing.

B. You are laughing.

A. You are laughing too.

B. I am laughing too.

A. You have stopped laughing.

B. I have stopped laughing.

A. You look sad.

B. I look sad.

A. You are sad.

B. I am sad.

A. You are sad.

B. You don't like that.

A. I don't like that.

This example has been condensed to give you a general idea. An exchange can run on for much longer with more repetitions of the same observation than I have included here.

If you do not agree with the observation, you can say, for example, 'No, I am not sad.' Your partner can either pick this up and repeat it or, if the behaviour that they are observing suggests it to them, they can reassert their initial observation. The main thing is to remain utterly truthful to what you observe and not invent things because it seems more interesting.

Here we are getting to the heart of this work. Meisner famously said, 'An ounce of behaviour is worth a tonne of words.'[2] So it is not *what* we say but *how* we say it that really matters. Think of all the underlying currents that can run through even the most banal conversation. As an example, in the following duologues I have put in square brackets what each person is picking up from the other's behaviour.

1.

'Would you like a cup of tea?' [You want to kiss me.]

'Yeah great thanks.' [You are frightened of being kissed by me.]

2.

'Would you like a cup of tea?' [You are going to cry.]

'Yeah great thanks.' [You don't know how to help me.]

3.

'Would you like a cup of tea?' [You are feeling lonely.]

'Yeah great thanks.' [You are befriending me.]

Try making your own scenarios up for similarly banal conversations. You will see that what is interesting does not lie with the words themselves, but the behaviour that informs them. As human beings, we respond to each other's behaviour; it makes sense that as actors we should also respond to the behaviour of those around us.

Be careful, though, that you do not *impose* anything on to this simple repetition exercise. React in proportion to the behaviour that is in front of you and do not assume something that you cannot see. As ever, do not try to be interesting. Listen, repeat, and engage with what is really going on in your partner and how that makes you feel.

Adding Layers

As with the previous exercises, work in pairs, labelling yourselves A and B.

A leaves the room and waits.

B is given a task to do, such as making a house out of cards or balancing a stick on her thumb; something physical and simple but requiring concentration to achieve.

A enters the space and the repetition exercise continues. This time, however, B also has the task to tackle. A will start by observing what she sees, for example: 'You are balancing a stick on your thumb.'

You can see that elements are gradually being added to the basic exercise, and these should provide you with further stimuli. As actor B, your need to engage in an activity while still responding to your partner will provoke a tension in you as you try to deal with the conflicting demands of the situation. As actor A, you will also be affected by your partner's activity; it will certainly give you some clear behaviour to respond to. Your partner's potential rejection of you in favour of the task may create conflict in you.

Another Layer

The exercise is as above. However, this time, as actor A, you have had time to choose your own task, and as actor B, you've had time to think of a reason for entering the room. In the previous exercise, actor B was given a task, and here actor A is being asked to choose one. The exercise should be done more than once, allowing each of you to have a turn at doing both the task and entering the room.

When you choose your task, make sure that it matters to you and that it is difficult to accomplish – but not impossible. You should bring everything you need into the class with you. For example:

- You might choose to mend a vase that you have smashed into several pieces. The vase might belong to your mother and be of sentimental value to her. She has no idea that you have broken it.

- You might need to learn a speech from *Hamlet* in preparation for an audition that you are going to in an hour. You really want to impress the director.

As for actor B, before you enter the room, you might decide that:

- You need a recipe for a complicated dish that only the other actor knows. You have told someone you want to impress that you will be cooking it for her that night.

- You need to get the other actor to babysit your four-year-old niece who you are in charge of. You want to go to a fantastic party instead. The little girl knows actor A and won't stay with anyone else.

You must be very specific, have thought about all the given circumstances surrounding your activity, and your reason for entering. You should allow yourself a credible timescale to achieve everything but not one that gives you much room for manoeuvre.

As actor B, you leave the room and allow your partner some time to engage in their activity.

Knock on the door and enter when actor A lets you in.

As with all the previous exercises in this section, you do not move on from the repetition until your partner's behaviour changes.

Here is a condensed example of what might happen:

Actor A is threading very small beads onto some cotton. She hears a knock on the door but is busy with her task. Actor B knocks again and this time A gets up to answer the door.

A (*opening the door*). You knocked loudly.

B. I knocked loudly. (*Entering the room.*)

A. You have walked in.

B. I have walked in.

A (*going back to her task*). You have walked in.

B. You are walking away from me.

A. I am walking away from you. (*Reaches the table where she was previously working and picks up the beads.*)

B. You are threading beads.

A. I am threading beads. (*Not looking up from her task.*)

B. You are ignoring me.

A. I am ignoring you.

B (*walks over to see what is going on*). You are ignoring me.

A. You are standing very close.

B. I am standing very close.

A (*looking directly at her partner*). You are standing very close!

B. It's annoying you… [*Etc.*]

As you can see, you are now working within a specific set of circumstances. You have purpose, but you must make sure that you are still responding to each other. Having entered, as actor B, you should focus on what is going on and not on the need that brought you there in the first place. That need simply gives you direction and informs your behaviour as you enter, beyond that it is not central to the exercise. This is important, because if you place all your attention on what you want you will miss what is happening in your partner. For actor A, the tension between the need to accomplish the task and the need to be in relation to your partner should really fuel you.

High Stakes

As above, one actor engages in a task, the other knocks and is let into the room.

This time, the stakes need to be raised much higher for both actors. The task should be one that you have an utterly pressing need to complete: the consequence of not doing so would be huge. Equally, your reason for coming into the room should be compelling. The exercise should be done more than once so that each of you has a chance to experience both engaging with the task, and entering the room.

Here is an example of situations where the stakes for both actors would be very high:

- Actor A is writing a funeral speech in memory of his brother, who has just died. He has to leave for the funeral in half an hour and he needs to find the exact words to express what his brother meant to him. He has not been able to begin the speech until now, and he knows he needs to do justice to his brother's memory.

- Actor B has just found out that her own brother has had an accident. She needs to get actor A to drive her to the hospital, which is in another city. He is the only person she knows with a car, she hasn't money for a cab and the next train doesn't leave for another four hours.

She doesn't know how bad her brother's condition is or how much time she has left to see him alive.

Neither of you should confer before you start. Use the repetition as you did during the previous exercises. Be very specific with all your given circumstances.

These scenarios are clearly traumatic, but you might equally choose something where the thing you need is wonderful. You might be preparing for a job of a lifetime, or you might think that you have won the lottery and that your partner has the ticket with the winning numbers on it. The point is that, either way, the stakes are extremely high. Do not hang on to the emotion that you are full of at the start of the exercise. Let yourself be altered by what your partner does to you, how their behaviour changes you. The person coming to the door needs to be emotionally full and will need to have prepared for this outside. As you enter, however, you must not work to hang on to that emotion. It brings you into the room and then you can leave it alone. Your inner life will be pulsating through you, so you can turn your attention to your partner and trust yourself to simply respond.

Use your imagination – you should not pick something that is actually happening to you because that would lead you into a different territory altogether and may cause you to lose control. Meisner said that acting is 'living truthfully under imaginary circumstances'.[3] Take a kernel of truth that you understand from your own life, and then build on it through your imagination. For instance, I know that I love my niece, I understand this to be true,

I can put her into all sorts of imaginary circumstances safe in the knowledge that she is absolutely fine.

You don't need to show us that you are churned up as a result of your imagination. Whatever life is going on inside you, you can leave it alone and trust that those emotions will breathe inside you without your having to work to keep them alive. The most important thing is that, having prepared fully, you observe your partner's behaviour very closely indeed, responding to everything that they do and allowing it to inform how you feel, and consequently alter your own behaviour.

All life is constantly changing. We are perpetually altering physically, the body you had yesterday is not quite the same as the one you own today. Not only that, but how we respond to a situation in one moment may completely contradict our behaviour in the next. We might think we will die if we are not loved by someone, but find that same person repellent when viewed in a different light. One generation fights an enemy that another allies itself with. We know that we are alive because we are constantly altering, because there is no fixed point. This work reflects this basic truth. It rebels against the sort of acting that tries to neatly pin behaviour down, to contain it – the sort of work where the actor is expected to plan meticulously for all events and, having done so, to never let that plan leave her hands. Of course, you need to prepare what material you have thoroughly, but beyond that you must be alive to what is happening in that moment as it occurs, and as it shapes your behaviour. If you know exactly what is coming and exactly what you are going to do every moment that you are onstage, then the audience will also know – and how boring is that, both for you and for them?

At the end of these sessions, it is hoped that you will have:

- The confidence to take the focus off yourself and to be really attentive to your partner.

- The habit of preparing given material thoroughly.

- The ability to let your imagination roam without censoring.

- The ability to explore without needing to reach a specific goal or to be 'impressive' to those watching.

The Significance of Objects

You have been working in response to each other as well as to the given circumstances that you have detailed during the exercises so far. Now you should consider another source of stimulus that you can add to the mix: the objects that you carry around with you and come into contact with.

Aims

- To use objects as a stimulus for emotional response.

- To further the idea that you don't have to dredge up emotion, but that it can be provoked by something outside of yourself.

- To encourage you to work in detail.

- To stimulate your imagination through endowment; attributing one thing with the qualities of another.

Don't Touch

You will have prepared for this session by choosing an object that has great significance for you. For example, a photograph, toy or book. It doesn't matter what you choose as long as you have a personal relationship with it. Do not choose something that means so much to you that that you cannot handle talking about it.

Introduce your object to the rest of the group. Describe it in great detail, the texture, smell, temperature, etc., as well as why it is significant to you and the story of how you came by it.

Think of a word or phrase that sums up your relationship with that object.

Place the object on the floor beside you. You may sit with it, lie by it, stand over it or walk around it, but you must not touch it and you must keep your focus on it.

After twenty minutes, you will be told that you can pick up your object if you wish to do so.

You can do this exercise simultaneously with the rest of the group; there is no need to watch each other.

This exercise encourages you to really pay attention to an object. It may feel silly sniffing a photograph, but you will notice so much more if you pay limitless amounts of attention to it. In a previous session you scrutinised your partner's face and observed details that you had previously missed, here we are doing the same thing, but with an object. Through noticing the details, you will gain a stronger relationship with that object and so will have more to respond to. Your senses will also be sharpened through the process.

Having really become acquainted with your object, it can be an interesting experience not to be able to touch it. I have seen actors grab at their object at the end of the exercise, but I have also seen others unable to pick theirs up even though they had previously loved it. The point is that when you stop thinking about yourself and really focus on the object it can trigger a whole raft of emotions in you. Remember to place your point of attention outside of yourself and then respond to what comes.

Endowment

Recall the word or phrase that you first came up with when you were asked in the previous exercise to sum up your relationship with your object. If this has changed as a result of the 'Don't Touch' exercise, think of a new word that expresses your current relationship with it. Spend some time with your object again, recalling how you came to acquire it and the memories associated with it, as well as reacquainting yourself with its physical attributes.

Put your own object to one side and choose another from a bag of miscellaneous things that has been brought in – things that have no particular significance for you.

Take some time to touch and smell this new object. Familiarise yourself with it thoroughly. Now recall your initial word or phrase, and endow the new object with the same significance as your old one had for you. In other words, imagine that the new object means the same to you as the old one.

Introduce this object to the rest of the group. Describe it in detail, explain why it is significant and relate the story behind it. Do not repeat the story attached to your initial object, come up with a new story for your new object. The words will be different but you will have endowed this object with the same significance as your own item had for you, your emotional responses will be similar to those triggered by the thing that you genuinely cared about. The only difference is that you are now talking about something that in reality you had no previous relationship with, although those listening should not be able to tell that.

From this exercise you should see that your imagination is incredibly powerful: through it you can endow any old thing with extraordinary qualities. It is all to do with you having a detailed and specific relationship with those things that you come into contact with.

Be careful that you pay attention to how you handle the objects and watch how other people do so. This work is not simply useful as a tool for connecting you to your emotions, it also encourages you to look for detail that could add texture within a scene. Perhaps you will be required to use an ashtray during some dialogue. How you flick your ash into a tin ashtray may be different to how you flick it into a crystal one passed down from your grandmother who you hated. Perhaps you will be required to sit in an armchair – might you sit differently if you knew that the man you love had just been settled there? Your choices will be justified by the given circumstances of the play, but you really need to pay attention to them. These details may not alter a scene hugely, but they will add credibility to it and keep you fresh as an actor. There is no need to demonstrate your relationship to an object, an audience may never need to know the history of the ashtray or the armchair – that can be your secret. The audience will pick up on and respond to a performance that is full of inner life.

As a result of this work you should:

- Be specific in the way that you relate to objects.

- Be able imaginatively to endow objects with qualities that you choose without them necessarily possessing those qualities originally.

- Be aware that a rich inner life can be stimulated in all sorts of ways that an audience doesn't necessarily need to know about.

Taking Action

Human beings are not simply responsive to one another, we also actively affect each other. We may want reassurance, money, status, sex, friendship – whatever it might be, it could be argued that every human exchange has at its heart the need to get something from the other person. Whether we are talking about the need for freedom or directions to the nearest station, in pursuit of either we affect those that we are dealing with and they us. This is a basic human dynamic and is present in all drama.

Aims

- To push you to continue working responsively.

- To encourage you to actively pursue an objective.

- To encourage you to work with high stakes.

- To engage your imagination.

- To help you to make the connection between the psychological and the physical.

- To encourage you to think in terms of overcoming obstacles.

Overcoming the Obstacle

You will be working with a partner and will have pre-pared for the exercise prior to the session.

Imagine a situation where you might really need some-thing from another person. Think of something that it would be hugely difficult for that other person to give you.

Here are some examples:

- I have borrowed £1000 from my flatmate. I was meant to have paid the money back weeks ago. My flatmate has now got into serious financial difficulties and has to have it back immediately. I need to persuade my mother to give me the money. I know that she is not well-off and that she has been saving up for months to take my dad away for their anniversary.

- I need my best friend to give me her blessing so that I can go out with her ex-boyfriend. I am besotted with him but unfortunately so is she!

- I am down to the last two for a good role in a major new film. My career would take off if I got the part. I know the other person that I am competing with and the job would change his life too. I need to convince him to drop out so that I become the front-runner.

In choosing your own scenario, pick something that you can relate to and that isn't an impossible ambition. Make sure that the stakes are high and you stand to gain a great deal if you are successful, but that you also stand to lose a great deal if you are not. Similarly, should you get what you want, it would be at a huge cost to the other person. As well as choosing an *objective*, consider your *super-objective*, i.e. the greater need under which the objective shelters and which informs it.

This exercise is done in pairs. Before the session, inform your partner of everything that they might need to know in order to engage fully with the improvisation that you will both be part of. They will obviously need to know what their relationship to you is, but also provide them with all the *given circumstances* involved; time, place, where they have just been, etc. If they need to know other factors, such as money being in short supply or that they are in love with someone, then tell them. Provide them with as much detail as possible without actually letting them know beforehand what your *objective* is – in other words, what the thing is that you need from them.

Having decided on your *objective*, think of three actions that you can do that would affect your partner so that they give you what you need. The physical and the psychological are not distinct; they cannot be separated.

In order to clarify what you are doing, use transitive verbs that describe each action. A transitive verb is a verb that requires a direct subject – in this case the other person is the direct subject. You are doing something *to* them. Here are examples of how you should use the verb. Obviously you are the 'I' in the sentence and your partner is the 'you'.

- I threaten you.
- I caress you.
- I shame you.

Some examples of verbs that are not transitive are 'die', 'wonder' and 'think'. Listen to how they sound and you will find that they don't make sense when used in the same way.

- I die you.

- I wonder you.

- I think you.

The exercise takes the form of an improvisation between you and your partner. Here is an example of a preparation for the improvisation.

Objective:
To stop my sister taking drugs.

Super-objective:
To save my family.

Given circumstances:
My sister is three years older than me. Despite being a heavy and regular user of ecstasy and cocaine, she manages to hold down her job as the manager of a restaurant. She enjoys her party lifestyle enormously and really resents anyone trying to tell her to make changes to it. Her boyfriend, who she is madly in love with, is also a serious drug-user, as are her friends. She has no desire whatsoever to quit the drugs. I can see that her addiction is becoming stronger and that her behaviour is taking its toll on our parents who are becoming ill with worry over her. Recently they have suspected that my sister has been stealing from them in order to finance her habit. No one has been able to get through to her. I believe that if I don't succeed in stopping her then the consequences will be cata-strophic. It is Saturday evening and my sister has just

got in from work. She is meeting her boyfriend in an hour's time. I have been at home all day trying to think of what to say to her. No one else is at home.

Actions (to 'my sister'):
- I befriend you.

- I shame you.

- I beg you.

You can bring in anything that you need in order to explore your actions fully. For instance, in order to *befriend* my sister I might bring her some food, I might paint her nails, I might brush her hair, I might play her some music, etc. To *shame* her I might produce a photo album stuffed with happy family photos and compare it to a picture of how our mother looks now. I might show her a letter that my father has written me, detailing his despair.

Whatever you do, you cannot rely on the words alone in order to get what you need. *How* you say what you say is of primary importance. What is your body doing that expresses the content of your speech? You may be asked to stop talking altogether and to investigate the action in purely physical terms. So if I am begging my sister, I might find myself lying at her feet grabbing on to her legs and kissing her feet! Do not worry about being subtle or original; the idea is to take the action as far as it will go without censorship.

Do not discard an action without exploring it fully. Actions can overlap and you can go back and forth between them, but you must engage in them whole-heartedly. The improvisation should last about fifteen minutes, and at any point during that time you can actually ask for whatever it is you need from the other person. If your partner gives you what you want, then that is the end of the exercise, as it means that through your actions you have achieved your objective. However, it doesn't matter if your partner does not give in, as the aim of the exercise is to push you to pursue actions fully, which you could do without your partner actually giving in to your demand – you have, after all, chosen something that is difficult for them. They are the *obstacle* you should try to overcome; whether you succeed is not the most important thing.

Be careful, do not forget all the previous work during which you responded to your partner's behaviour. This is an improvisation, and although you have prepared for it, it is not rehearsed. You cannot know what your partner will do so you need to constantly adapt your actions in response to what you are getting back from them. It may be that other actions emerge during the course of the improvisation. Do not cling rigidly to what you have planned. You are engaging in an exchange between human beings, and that is a fluid thing. The actions you have to work with are a scaffold from which the improvisation hangs, but then anything can happen.

Be imaginative with your transitive verbs and do not pick things that might rely too heavily on words alone. For instance, 'I flatter you' can easily descend into a list of adjectives describing how great the other person is. Words that are not somehow embodied physically and that do not inform your behaviour are empty vessels. If you do want to choose 'I flatter you', then think of physical ways of engaging with it. For example, you could draw a picture of your partner or dress up like them or mirror their physicality in some way. You might find some verbs harder to explore than others, such as 'I persuade you' or 'I convince you' are not suitable. They are very general and one can always ask the question, how are you going to do that? In what way are you going to convince or persuade her? Think outside of the box! There are so many transitive verbs to choose from. 'I beg you', 'I threaten you' and 'I scare you' might serve you very well, but then again so might 'I squeeze you', 'I prod you' or 'I cradle you.'

Do be careful of what you choose, however, as you will be expected to explore your action thoroughly. I have seen actors set out to seduce their partners only to find that when the chips are down they become rather shy. Remember that it is your own interpretation of the verb – there isn't only one way of seducing someone. That action can take many forms!

Because you are working with very high stakes, you are exploring the actions in a way that is heightened and that pushes you to take the exercise to extremes. When you use actions in relation to text you will pursue them to varying degrees, but here you are given the chance to really experience fully what it is to play an action. We employ actions in order to change people to get what we need, but we also respond to what they do to us in return. Our partners will be playing actions too. Since this is the case, as a result of this work you should:

- Understand the need to be flexible and spontaneous.

- Be able to work boldly and without censorship.

- Be able to fully engage and focus on your purpose.

- Understand that the psychological has a physical expression and that the physical has psychological consequences.

The Obstacle Within

This work continues to explore tensions between your objective and whatever it is that prevents you from achieving it. In the previous exercise you worked with a partner; they served as the obstacle that you had to overcome in order to gain your objective. Now the need and its obstruction will coexist within you.

Aims

- To experience what it feels like to be pulled in two directions.

- To have a sense of the world outside of the room in which your scenario takes place.

Pulled in Two Directions

You must prepare for this exercise, but you should not rehearse it. You will need to bring in any objects that you require, not only to use during the session but also, if needed, to make the space feel more familiar to you – for example, pictures, cushions, rugs, etc. There will already be a bed set up for you to use.

This exercise is again done in pairs. Your partner lies in the bed as if they are asleep. Use your imagination to substitute your partner for someone else. Choose someone to whom you have a very strong attachment and who you would find it extremely difficult to leave in the particular circumstances that you are going to create. This person can be anyone, a parent, lover, sibling or friend; it doesn't matter as long as you really care about them. The stakes must be very high.

Think of an extremely pressing reason to leave. Your objective must relate to the world outside of the room and should be absolutely compelling.

Make sure that you have considered all the *given circumstances* involved. The time is already established for you, it is two o'clock in the morning. Your sleeping partner must be told prior to the beginning of the exercise what their relationship to you is.

Begin the exercise lying beside your partner. When you are ready, get out of the bed and start doing three tasks that need to be accomplished in order for you to leave the room. Make sure that they are active and that they take some time to complete. For example, reading is not physically active enough and putting on a pair of socks is too simple, although getting fully dressed for a specific encounter or purpose would be suitable.

Your partner will wake if you make too much noise. You will need to be quiet, though your partner should not be listening out for every tiny creak in the floorboards. They should respond only to what would reasonably disturb them. If your partner wakes up they will ask you what you are doing, and you will then have a choice: you can either climb back into bed with them, or explain what you are up to. Any ensuing improvisation is not hugely relevant within the context of this exercise. Engaging with the activities, having a strong objective and an equally powerful obstacle are.

You may find that your sleeping partner is too much of an obstacle and that you do not succeed in leaving the room, or you may not. Until you finish the exercise you cannot know its outcome. Just make sure that the objective pulls you away and that the reason for staying is equally compelling. Take a core truth and build on it with your imagination. Do not use events that are actually happening to you in real life.

In order to clarify this exercise so that you can see how it might work in practice, here are two examples for you.

Lucy's Exercise

Given circumstances:
Lucy is in bed with John. He is her boyfriend. She has been with him for five years and loves him very deeply. It is two o'clock in the morning. It is December and it is very cold. They are in the bedroom of the flat that they share and that John loves. Lucy has been using credit and store cards to spend wildly on clothes, furniture for the flat, an exotic holiday and a deposit on a car, and her debts are now overwhelming. Her creditors are calling in their loans. Her boyfriend has no idea that they are three months behind on the rent. He is a student and has little money. Lucy is in charge of paying the rent, and now her landlord has told her that they will be evicted from the flat if the rent isn't paid by the weekend. She is frightened that, if her boyfriend finds out what she has done and they get kicked out, he will end the relationship. This is an unbearable thought for her. She has no one to borrow the money from, but her boss, who she knows has always fancied her, has offered to stump up the cash if she has sex with him. Having agreed to the bargain, she now fears that she may lose her job altogether if she doesn't go

through with it. She has agreed to go to her boss's house that night, but she has had to wait till the small hours as her boyfriend has taken so long to fall asleep. She has to go straight on to work after she has been with her boss.

Objective:
To go and sleep with her boss to get the money for the rent.

Super-objective:
To save her relationship.

Obstacle:
Her boyfriend would be horrified and devastated by her behaviour and she loves him very much. Unlike her boyfriend, her boss is not particularly attractive to her.

Activities:
• Getting dressed in her outfit for work.

• Putting on make-up.

• Preparing a breakfast tray for her boyfriend with croissants and orange juice and a flower and a note that she writes in order to explain that she has gone to work early, so that when he wakes in the morning for college he won't wonder where she is.

Michael's Exercise

Given circumstances:
Michael lies beside Flora, his mother. It is two o'clock on a spring morning. The air is warm despite the sun not yet having risen. They are in the hospital where Michael has been staying for the past three weeks. His mother is seriously ill following an accident, and the doctors don't know if, let alone when, she will recover. Michael has an

extremely strong relationship with his mother, whom he loves very much. He has barely left her bedside and has brought clothes and books and papers to the room so that he wouldn't have to leave it to go and collect things from his flat, which is quite a distance away. Prior to the accident, Michael auditioned to play Hamlet in a production that is to tour the US for six months. He was offered the part and accepted the job immediately. Rehearsals start in America in two days' time. His flight is booked for ten o'clock that morning. The job is exciting, prestigious and well paid. Playing the role of Hamlet is an opportunity that may never come his way again. He has been struggling to work consistently as an actor, and this job offers an almost miraculous career break for him.

Objective:
To get to the airport to catch a plane to New York.

Super-objective:
To be a great actor.

Obstacle:
If he goes he might never see his mother again.

Activities:
- To pack a bag with all the belongings he has there that he will need for the trip, and to sort through the things that he has amassed during his stay that he will not be taking.

- To make a collage of photos of him and his mother together in the hope that she will see it when she wakes up.

- To write his mother a letter explaining how much he loves her and his reasons why he has to leave.

As you can see, these scenarios hold very high stakes for both Lucy and Michael. Lucy's core truth was that she loved her boyfriend and she built imaginary circumstances that might threaten her relationship with him. For Michael, his ambition was the core truth and he imagined circumstances that might impede his progress as an actor. Both of them found the exercise very emotional, but neither settled into their emotion, nor held on to it. They fought how they were feeling in order to pursue their objectives. Their needs kept them moving forward. When you do an exercise like this, let everything that you do have a ripple effect, as one moment touches and alters the next. If you work in this way then you will not fall into a state of generalised emotion and find yourself unable to climb out of it, regardless of the given circumstances.

As a result of the conflict, you should experience tension throughout your whole body, and this will be accentuated by your need to keep quiet as you engage in your activities. Those watching should be able to see your struggle expressed physically, not simply through your facial expressions or through any tears that you might shed. What makes this work exciting for those watching is that they do not know what choice you are going to make. What actually happened in the examples that I have outlined here was that Lucy got back into bed with her boyfriend and Michael left to get on the plane. But nobody, including the actors, knew the outcomes beforehand.

Later, when you work with text, where the playwright will have decided for you whether you leave the room or not, the *way* in which you do so can be informed by the contradictions and opposing needs that the character experiences. Even if you are playing Hamlet and your entire audience knows that ultimately his choices lead to disaster, those watching need to feel that just this once, perhaps, he will take a different route and meet another fate. We need to believe that it isn't preordained that he behaves as he does; there are different urges going on inside of him and a different outcome would have been possible if he had followed an alternative path. If the actor doesn't engage with the alternative path then the play loses much of its resonance.

By exploring the contradictory forces you become physically alive and far more complex emotionally. You will find layers in your work that will add texture and detail. This exercise also encourages you to expand imaginatively as you take into account the world outside of the room, as well as those things that occupy the space within it. Be careful to choose scenarios that draw on this imagination. Take a core truth, such as the love you feel for your mother, and then create a set of circumstances around this. Do not try to explore a situation that is really happening to you. Keep playful and creative.

As a result of the work you will have:

- Experienced physically the push and pull of contradicting needs.

- Worked with an obstacle that remains silent so that the voice that interferes with the objective speaks from within you, creating an internal struggle.

- Worked without anticipating the result of the exercise.

- Continued to work imaginatively and responsively.

Working with Text

The sort of plays that you are likely to work on at this stage of your training will be, broadly speaking, naturalistic. The emphasis of the first year is still very much on the self. You are bringing yourself to the text.

Aims

- To offer tools for organising the text so that you can make sense of what is going on within it.

- To enable you to deliver the text purposefully.

- To encourage you to make your own choices without losing sight of the playwright's intentions.

- To look at ways in that will help you to find a personal connection with the text.

- To encourage you to approach the text imaginatively and with creativity.

Unpacking the Narrative

Having read the play carefully several times, make a list of all the events that take place in it that you think are essential in order for the story to be told.

Present a 'potted version' of each act of the play showing these crucial events. You can do this in any way you like, using text, tableaux, rhythm, movement, etc. To help to make this sound less daunting for you, I will give you an example of my own potted version of the beginning of Act One of *The Crucible* by Arthur Miller, so that you can see what I mean.

- Reverend Parris prays and weeps over his daughter Betty who lies, unmoving, on the bed.

- Tituba, his slave from Barbados, enters to see if Betty is all right. Parris throws her out.

- Abigail, Parris's niece, enters to tell her uncle that Susannah is here to see him, having been to talk to the doctor.

- Susannah tells Parris that the doctor can't find any natural causes for Betty's condition.

- Parris announces that he has sent for Reverend Hale to come and confirm that there are no unnatural causes behind Betty's sudden inability to move; that she is not under the spell of witchcraft.

- Abigail tells Parris that rumours about witchcraft are going round the village, and that he ought to go and talk to all the people who have now come to the house, and tell them that the rumours are untrue. Parris refuses to do this.

- Abigail admits to her uncle that she and other girls, including Betty, were dancing in the forest, but insists that they were not conjuring spirits. She explains that when Parris came upon them, Betty had simply fainted in fright.

- Parris refuses to believe it and, fearing for his standing in the village, and reprisals from his enemies if his own daughter has been involved in anything scandalous or sinful, keeps pressing for the truth. He says that he saw Tituba waving her arms over the fire and screeching. He says, with great difficulty, that he also saw a dress on the floor and someone running naked through the trees.

- Parris asks Abigail whether there is any other reason, apart from those he already knows, that would explain why Goody Proctor had sacked her, and why she won't come to church regularly any more for fear of coming close to Abigail. Abigail explains that Goody Proctor is a mean, cold woman, who hates her for refusing to be her slave. She accuses Goody Proctor of being a liar.

Through this process you should start to become aware of how the narrative of the play unfolds. You will have defined where you think the dramatic moments fall and the story moves on. It is very useful as a way of noting what is actually being done in each beat of the text. Be careful, however, as it is easy to include too many moments as being pivotal and so start cluttering up the narrative spine with interesting but not necessarily essential events. The point of this exercise is to take a clear look at the play as a whole, and to begin to relate to it in its simplest form. Be strict with yourself: only include events on your list without which the play could not take place. Discussion will arise as to quite what these events might be and there may be some disagreement, but this is a good thing as the debate will push you to look at the dramaturgy very closely. In other words, you will have to look closely at how the play is structured.

Changing Chairs

Take a scene from the play you are looking at, preferably a duologue. Certainly, to begin with, there should be no more than three characters involved.

While the rest of the group make a wide circle with their chairs, in the centre place a chair for each of the actors in the scene, plus an extra one.

Each actor decides before they begin reading what their character's objective is at the start of the scene. They need to establish what they think their character needs at that point. This is only an initial idea, put forward by the actor and shared with the rest of the group; it may well change as a result of working on the scene more closely.

Start reading the scene together out loud. When you think your own character's objective changes, then move to sit on the unoccupied chair. Each actor involved in the scene will move chairs when they think that their objective changes.

When you have established that there is a shift, underline this in your script. By doing this you will divide the scene up into sections that begin and end with a change of objective. You can call these sections *units*. Give each unit a title that explains what the objective is from your character's point of view. Even though it is likely that characters may well have units in common, they will not share the same titles for those units.

Here is an example to help you to get a clearer picture. I will look at a section of Act Two, Scene One from Arthur Miller's play *The Crucible*. Before you go on, it is important that you understand that, though I have divided the text up in this way, when you come to do it you might see things differently – there are no hard-and-fast rules. As you begin to work, you will discover all sorts of shifts within the scene. There will be tangents and distractions, fascinating details, but be careful not to overcomplicate matters. Acknowledge the detours as they will texture your work, but do not move from your seat unless your actual objective has changed, i.e. unless your character wants something other than they did previously. You will generally find that an objective will change if a character leaves or another enters because then the whole dynamic of the scene is forced to shift, and so you with it. Just as with the previous exercise, it is very easy to overdo it. I have seen actors begin what looks like a dance as they leap up every time that they speak. The point is that, by breaking up the text in this way, you create a pathway for yourself, enabling you to see the scene more clearly. Once you have understood *what* is going on in a scene, then you can begin to look at *how* it is happening and *why*. Working like this gives you the opportunity to look at one section at a time in detail, rather than become overwhelmed by the whole. You will begin too, to get a measure of the rhythms in the text as you map out the shifts.

I have placed a line where I think that both characters would change chairs, and included each actor's objective for each unit in square brackets.

[*Elizabeth needs her husband to go to Salem to tell the authorities that Abigail is lying.*

Proctor needs to think it over before he accuses Abigail of fraud.]

ELIZABETH. I think you must go to Salem, John.

He turns to her.

I think so. You must tell them it is a fraud.

PROCTOR (*thinking beyond this*). Aye, it is, it is surely.

ELIZABETH. Let you go to Ezekiel Cheever – he knows you well. And tell him what she said to you last week in her uncle's house. She said it had naught to do with witchcraft, did she not?

PROCTOR (*in thought*). Aye, she did, she did.

Now, a pause.

ELIZABETH (*quietly, fearing to anger him by prodding*). God forbid you keep that from the court, John. I think they must be told.

PROCTOR (*quietly, struggling with his thought*). Aye, they must, they must. It is a wonder they do believe her.

ELIZABETH. I would go to Salem now, John – let you go tonight.

PROCTOR. I'll think on it.

ELIZABETH (*with her courage now*). You cannot keep it, John.

PROCTOR (*angering*). I know I cannot keep it. I say I will think on it!

ELIZABETH (*with her courage now*). Good, then let you think on it.

[*Elizabeth needs to retreat.*

Proctor needs to keep her with him.]

   She stands and starts to walk out of the room.

PROCTOR. I am only wondering how I may prove what she told me, Elizabeth. If the girl's a saint now, I think it is not easy to prove she's a fraud, and the town gone so silly. She told it to me in a room alone – I have no proof for it.

_____

[*Elizabeth needs to establish the truth.*

Proctor needs to tell her that it was nothing to worry about.]

ELIZABETH. You were alone with her?

PROCTOR (*stubbornly*). For a moment alone, aye.

ELIZABETH. Why, then, it is not as you told me.

PROCTOR (*his anger rising*). For a moment, I say. The others come in soon after.

_____

[*Elizabeth needs to withdraw from him.*

Proctor needs to make her stay.]

ELIZABETH (*quietly – she has suddenly lost all faith in him*). Do as you wish, then. (*She starts to turn.*)

PROCTOR. Woman.

_____

[*Proctor needs Elizabeth to stop doubting him.*

Elizabeth needs to make him see that she has reason to doubt.]

She turns to him.

I'll not have your suspicion any more.

ELIZABETH (*a little loftily*). I have no –

PROCTOR. I'll not have it!

ELIZABETH. Then let you not earn it.

PROCTOR (*with a violent undertone*). You doubt me yet?

ELIZABETH (*with a smile, to keep her dignity*). John, if it were not Abigail that you must go to hurt, would you falter now? I think not.

PROCTOR. Now look you –

ELIZABETH. I see what I see, John.

PROCTOR (*with solemn warning*). You will not judge me more, Elizabeth. I have good reason to think before I charge fraud on Abigail, and I will think on it. Let you look to your own improvement before you go to judge your husband any more. I have forgot Abigail, and –

ELIZABETH. And I.

––––––––––––––––

[*Proctor needs to put an end to the way their relationship has been for the past seven months.*

Elizabeth needs to justify herself.]

PROCTOR. Spare me! You forget nothin' and forgive nothin'. Learn charity, woman. I have gone tiptoe in this house all seven month since she is gone. I have not moved from there to there without I think to please you, and still an everlasting funeral marches round your heart. I cannot speak but I am doubted, every moment judged for lies, as though I come into a court when I come into this house!

ELIZABETH. John, you are not open with me. You saw her with a crowd, you said. Now you –

PROCTOR. I'll plead my honesty no more, Elizabeth.

ELIZABETH (*now she would justify herself*). John, I am only –

PROCTOR. No more! I should have roared you down when first you told me your suspicion. But I wilted, and, like a Christian, I confessed. Confessed! Some dream I had must have mistaken you for God that day. But you're not, you're not, and let you remember it! Let you look sometimes for the goodness in me, and judge me not.

ELIZABETH. I do not judge you. The magistrate sits in your heart that judges you. I never thought you but a good man, John – (*With a smile.*) only somewhat bewildered.

PROCTOR (*laughing bitterly*). Oh, Elizabeth, your justice would freeze beer!

Applying Transitive Verbs to Text

When you have divided the scene into sections, take one unit at a time and for each sentence within it choose a transitive verb that you think reflects what you are doing to your onstage partner. (If you need to remind yourself about transitive verbs look back at the section 'Taking Action'.)

Say the transitive verb and then say the line accordingly.

Again using *The Crucible*, here are examples of what I mean:

ELIZABETH (*quietly*). [*I shake you.*] Oh, the noose, the noose is up!

PROCTOR. [*I steady you.*] There'll be no noose.

ELIZABETH. [*I stir you.*] She wants me dead. [*I reproach you.*] I knew all week it would come to this!

PROCTOR (*without conviction*). [*I reassure you.*] They dismissed it. [*I remind you.*] You heard her say –

ELIZABETH. [*I push you.*] And what of tomorrow? [*I beg you.*] She will cry me out until they take me!

PROCTOR. [*I control you.*] Sit you down.

ELIZABETH. [*I clutch you.*] She wants me dead, John, you know it!

PROCTOR. [*I order you.*] I say sit down!

Work through the whole text in this way.

Go through each section again, but this time another actor will read your lines for you; you are no longer responsible for the actual words. The actor reading should do so in a neutral way, so that they are not imposing choices on you as they speak the text. As the lines are read out, physicalise the transitive verb, so that instead of speaking the text, you actually *do* whatever it is to the other person. Each actor in the scene should have someone reading their lines for them. Take it to its absolute extreme. For example, instead of saying 'I worry you', followed by the line, you might express this by curling up into a tight ball and rocking from side to side so that your fellow actors cannot help but be affected by you. Do what ever you want without stopping to think about it.

When you have been through the scene, return to the text itself and speak the lines as written, without stating the verb or physicalising it. Use the words themselves to explore the action, and notice how they are affected by the previous exercises.

Be very careful with this work. I have seen actors who get so hung up finding the right transitive verb that they become blocked by the struggle. They stop doing anything to anyone else and become totally head-bound as they try to come up with absolutely the best word that they can. Finding transitive verbs to express the action is a tool only; the process offers you a way of seeing what you are doing in relation to others in the scene and in relation to your character's needs, it is not an end in itself. Do not get preoccupied by chasing a word, it is more important that you just keep exploring actively. If you can't define something with absolute precision, just get on and do it as best you can without worrying about what to call it. When you worry you stop listening.

I have also seen actors become very rigid with this work. I have seen them hold on to their actions regardless of what else is happening in the scene. Despite a shift in dynamic or in another character's behaviour, they carry on playing whatever they had previously decided to play when they first considered the transitive verbs. If you work like this, what you produce will be dead. By holding on too tightly to your action word, you create a bubble around you, which prevents you from being able to relate to your fellow actors, and because you are in this bubble you cannot respond to what is happening at that moment. You must keep listening and reacting. A transitive verb or action will stop making sense if it bears no relation to what another character is doing to you, or to the given circumstances of the scene. Think about catching a butterfly and holding it in your hands. If you hold it too tightly you will kill it. Working with transitive verbs is a means by which to move forward, but it is not the purpose of the scene. Do not let the exercise stifle your creativity.

Another very important thing to consider is how forcefully you are playing the action. In the part of the exercise in which you were asked to physicalise the verb, you were instructed to take things as far as you could; this was so that you could understand what it is to be fully in the action using your entire body, without just functioning from the neck up. As you become more aware of the need to effect change in other people, start to consider to what extent you are playing the action; this will avoid generalisation. You may be going all out to seduce someone, or you may be gently flirting. In exploration take things to the extreme, but be aware that the force of your playing ultimately needs to be justified by the given circumstances of the text.

If you do get caught up in your head, come back to what is being done to you – focus entirely on the other person.

Making Choices

Write a short exchange between two people. Since this will not have been taken from a larger bit of text, it cannot be placed into a wider context, so you have less to focus on. Here is an example:

A. How are you?

B. I am fine.

A. Is that book any good?

B. Yes it is.

A. Have you read it before?

B. Yes I have.

Read the dialogue with your partner without making any choices. Now consider what you would do to make the text come alive. Remember the questions that came up during the section 'You Are Enough'.

- Who would I like to be?

- Who am I afraid that I might be?

- Where am I?

- When is it?

- Where have I just been?

- What do I need?

- What gets in the way of me getting what I need?

- How am I going to get over what stands in my way?

- Where am I going next?

- What is my relationship with the other person?

- Why now?

Work through the dialogue answering these questions. You will both need to agree on the answers that involve a shared sense of time, space and relationship, but there is no reason why you should work everything out together. As you play the scene, tensions may reveal themselves that will inject it with life and make it far more interesting than it may appear on first reading.

Having done this, work through a short scene that you have not written yourself, with a partner.

Here are a few examples of the sort of texts that would be appropriate:

- *On the Shore of the Wide World* by Simon Stephens (Scene One).

- *Some Voices* by Joe Penhall (Act One, Scene Two).

- *Cold* by David Mamet.

- *Made of Stone* by Leo Butler (Scene One or Scene Five).

- *Country Music* by Simon Stephens (Act One).

Think about what the playwright's intentions might be, but at the same time notice the wealth of choices available to you.

Apply the above questions to the text.

Look for the shifts in objectives.

Consider what the characters are actually *doing* to each other.

Be imaginative!

Keep in mind that your choices must be justified by a clear process in which you have asked specific questions of the text. The inspiration for your choices should come out of an idea of what the script is doing, rather than from an attempt to impose dramatic qualities on it that will please the actor, but not serve the piece.

I have been asked by actors if there is any point in them actively making choices when the writer is going to do the work for them anyway? If it was the case that actors relied only on what the playwright told them to do, and never put their own slant on things, then all scripts would be delivered in the same way – and we know from seeing many different productions of the same piece that this is not the case. An actor is responsible for joining up all the clues that the writer has left in order to tell the story. Indeed, the actor is often responsible for deciding what the clues are in the first place.

The choices you make will depend on the text you are working on. The structure of the play and the dramatic moments contained in it need to be considered carefully, but you also need to consider your response to that text. You need to make the text your own and to view its landscape through the eyes of your character. Once you trust that you understand the script and its structure, and have asked the relevant questions of it, you will know that the choices you make will be justified. These choices will not come out of a random desire to experiment for the sake of it, but instead from a thorough deciphering of the codes of the text, and then an interpretation of what you have found. Do not wait to be told what to do, always bring something to the table. Make choices – they can easily be discarded in favour of new ones, and it is easier to take ideas away than to make something from nothing.

Free Association

Read the play at least three times.

In this exercise, as an example, I have used Olga from Anton Chekhov's *Three Sisters*. (I have used Stephen Mulrine's translation published by Nick Hern Books.) You will write three lists:

a. Everything you say about yourself.

'I think I'd have done better, if I'd got married and stayed home all day.'

b. Everything the other characters say about you.

(i.e. Kulygin, her sister's husband): 'You know, I often think, if it hadn't been for Masha, I should've married you. You're so kind.'

c. Everything you say about the other characters.

(i.e. Baron Tuzenbakh, who wants to marry her sister): 'After all you respect him, you think highly of him... True, he's not good looking, but he's a decent man, clean-living...'

What, at this stage, do you feel is your character's *super-objective* (deeper wish/spine phrase)? In other words, the absolute bottom line of need, the bigger desire that drives you to act and behave as you do.

For example, again using Olga from *Three Sisters*, I might explore the idea that her deeper wish is to escape her present life by getting married. I may change my mind about this being her super-objective as I continue to work on the play, but it is a useful starting point.

Go through the whole text and write down all the key phrases that your character speaks (i.e. the things that are of true importance to them).

Use the exact words that the playwright has given the character. If the context is unclear, then write in brackets beside the line what the character is referring to.

Here are some examples taken from Olga's point of view.

- 'Father died exactly a year ago, this very day.'

- 'We can talk about it [*his death*] quite calmly.'

- 'I can remember so well, how everything's already in flower in Moscow by this time, the beginning of May, how warm it is, everything bathed in sunshine.'

- '[*I felt*] Such an intense longing to go home.'

- 'To tell you the truth, these past four years I've been teaching at the high school, it's as if all my strength and youth have been ebbing away, drop by drop.'

- 'To Moscow, as soon as possible!'

From these key phrases, select what you consider to be the most provocative statements. These are the lines that provoke *you*, i.e. phrases that you as an actor have a gut reaction to. Choose one and write it at the top of a sheet of paper.

Close your eyes and say the provocative statement over and over to yourself until it starts to have an effect on you. When this happens, open your eyes and, under where you have originally written it down, write a free association that follows on from that statement. Use 'I' not the character's name. What you write should be informed by your close reading of the whole script, but there are no rules: any image, thought, feeling that arises should be written without self-censorship. Fill the page without pausing. Do it quickly and do not use any punctuation. In effect, you are committing to paper a stream of consciousness triggered by the phrase.

This is what I came up with following on from the key phrases that I picked out for Olga earlier:

'[*I felt*] Such a longing for home.'

I woke up early and the light was coming in through the window and it reminded me of the light at home and my bedroom there with its white walls and book-shelf and neat bed with the cotton quilt on it Father is downstairs but my sisters are still asleep it is quiet but I can feel Moscow stirring around me waking up great buildings the river cafés full of life people to talk to my home so safe there but with a world outside of its blue door a world of men and of people who are educated the garden is green and there are some roses in it they are full and honey-coloured in summer there is cherry blossom everywhere white and pink and I can cup the flowers and feel how soft they are in my hands the scruffy cat who wanders in for scraps of food the stove that gives off so much heat in the winter when it snows the armchair my father sits in and the lamp that makes the sitting room glow a little my desk dark wood where I study photographs of Mama on the piano.

Now go through the script again and this time, write down all the key facts. These are the people, places and things that are significant in the life of your character.

Here are some examples for Olga in *Three Sisters*:

- Irina's name-day

- Snow

- The clock

- The band playing at my father's funeral

- Rain

- The birch trees

- Moscow

- Spring

- School

Underneath each key fact, write down everything your character says about that fact. When you have done this, take one of the facts and read everything that you have written about it several times until it starts to work on you. When this happens, write a free association directly underneath as you did with the provocative statements. This time, just write one or two paragraphs. You can add to these paragraphs at a later date.

Remember to return to the key facts and phrases during further work on the text. Revisiting them will bring up different associations each time, and so keep your connection to what you are saying fresh and specific.

The idea behind this work is that you need to really get under the skin of your character; you need to understand the world from your character's perspective. When you talk, you need to know about the things that are significant to your character.

It is important that, once you have done this work, you do not actively try to bring it into rehearsals. Trust that it will have fuelled your inner life and your imagination. You will be filled with feelings and images, and these will reveal themselves in how you move, touch, speak and respond, etc., without your having to call them up deliberately. Your words will have an impulse behind them that will make them vivid for an audience. You must resist the temptation to try to force all that inner life to the surface in order to display it to those watching. If you do, your focus will be on yourself rather than on all those things around you that populate your character's world and influence their actions.

This work goes against the need for you to write a character biography. I have known actors who have faithfully written out lengthy histories for their characters. These might include the name of the hospital they were born in, what they like to eat for breakfast, where they went to school, etc. Much of what they write will be created for the sake of it, and it will do nothing to make the actual dialogue dance, or aid them in reaching a deeper understanding of the script. On the other hand, the exercises I have suggested draw directly from the text and demand that you, the actor, start to look through your character's eyes, and understand fully and specifically what you are talking about. This is far more valuable than the dutiful process of writing character biographies. The actor should do and feel, not think and record.

Freedom to Play

Having read the script at least three times, write a monologue for your character.

The action in the monologue should take place at any time during the year that precedes the start of the play.

During the monologue you must not mention any of the other characters by name, although of course they may be referred to indirectly.

Do not write a list of facts simply outlining things that have happened. Instead, your speech should look at an *experience* that your character has undergone or is undergoing and should not simply be a *description* of the event.

For instance, if I am looking at the character of Yelena from *Uncle Vanya* by Anton Chekhov: from my reading of the play, I understand that she is locked into a marriage that stifles her and is excited by the presence of a man who is younger and more interesting to her than her husband is. Perhaps, then, I might write a monologue recalling a bath that I took just after this man has left the house, a week before the play starts. I have been fantasising about meeting him in the forest, although even the thought of this terrifies me. I recall the temperature of the water, the touch of the flannel on my skin, etc. Notice that I am referring to these experiences in the first person. As you do this exercise, you need to try and climb right inside the experience that you are talking about. You can see from this example that the monologue you write is informed by what you have discovered from reading the play.

As you write your monologue, think of five characteristics that you think your character might possess. For example, I think Yelena is bored, sensual, lonely, creative and fearful. She is most likely a lot of other things aside from these, but they are good starting points for me to experiment with, and will help me get going. When you go through your monologue, try to explore the characteristics you have chosen physically. For instance:

- How does the character sit or stand?

- Where in their body do they hold tension?

- What are their rhythms both inner and outer?

- What is their point of concentration?

This exercise not only encourages you to view the world of the play through the eyes of your character, it should also help make you familiar with the text. You should have a specific relationship with and attitude towards events within the play, since whatever you choose to write about is informed by what you have discovered from the script itself. Writing the monologue requires you to be creative and playful. I really urge you to work from a place of exploration rather than a desire to achieve results: because the monologue is a product of your personal reading of the play, it is not a matter of getting things right or wrong. Be imaginative: as long as you rely on the text to justify your choices, the potential for creativity and exploration is exciting.

Breathing the Text

Take a monologue or batch of lines from the script you are working on. Starting from the beginning and working through to the end, read the text to yourself, focusing on small sections at a time. It could be that you read a word only or a sentence or a phrase. Stop reading further as soon as your attention has been caught.

At this point, start to breathe in and out steadily whilst going over this fragment of the text to yourself.

When an image or feeling comes to you, exhale and then speak the section of text out loud – but make sure it is informed by that image or emotion.

Do not try to make sense of what comes out, but commit to it fully. Do not contextualise it or attempt to make it fit with the meaning of the play as a whole.

When you have spoken the word or words in this way, do not revisit them. Start breathing in and out as you read over your next snippet of text. When you feel yourself connecting to something, then exhale and speak that section of text out loud.

Go through all your text in this way. You can move about as you do so, or you can stay quite still, whichever you find works best for you.

When you have gone through the whole thing, then simply read all the lines out loud and register any differences.

Although this work derives from the ideas of renowned acting coach Harold Guskin,[4] you might struggle to trust it to begin with. You may well have the urge to rush through it or to impose logic onto it. Once you stop trying to rationalise the process, however, you might be very surprised by some of the things that you discover in the text as a result of doing the exercise. Actors often enjoy a wonderful sense of abandon and liberation during the process. In order to experience this yourself, you need to ignore any of those deadly inner voices that question or censor or judge you, at least during the exercise itself. Of course, these voices should be ignored throughout your training, but this is harder to do in some situations than in others. You will need to guard against them throughout your time at drama school and beyond. If you can work with openness here, then you should find that an image, which may seem to surface randomly, will on reflection serve to illuminate a layer of meaning within the text or to offer a useful insight into the character's inner workings.

Each version of the speech is also now made very personal to the actor delivering it. You might find this useful in a number of ways. You should find that your subconscious has been liberated, which will make the text more lively and unpredictable to those receiving it. You can continue to use the exercise to refresh yourself during a long run. Each time you breathe in and out, different feelings and images will impact on you so the piece will not get stale. You might also use this exercise in preparation for an audition, because, as the process makes the speech personal to you, you will discover a unique relationship to it and will not deliver a repetition of what other actors may have done with the same speech.

As a result of this work it will be expected that:

- You engage with the text in a way that serves the play as a whole and tells its story.

- You are specific and detailed in your choices.

- You constantly work in relation to what you are doing to those around you in the scene.

- You do not merely present the emotion of the scene.

- You make a personal connection to the text so that it becomes vivid and unpredictable for those watching.

- You are fluid and responsive in the way that you work.

Character

You will have seen previously that the word 'character' has cropped up regularly. All the exercises have in fact been working to engage your imagination, chip away at blocks and offer tools so that, ultimately, you will be able to create a character more effectively. This section focuses directly on exercises that relate to a role that you might be playing.

Aims

- To recognise the complex and often contradictory forces that exist within a character.

- To consider the character in a context that is not explored directly during the play itself.

- To explore ways of gaining a deeper understanding of the character.

- To engage your imagination.

- To consider some of the physical properties of your character.

Multiple Personalities

Write a list of qualities that you think the character you are playing possesses. In order to do this, look at what your character says, but also how he behaves. Similarly, look at what the other characters say about him and also how they behave around him. You might find it useful to write the three lists as you did earlier in the 'Free Association' exercise, detailing what you say about yourself, what you say about others, and what others say about you.

We looked at part of a scene from *The Crucible* by Arthur Miller in the previous section, so let's return to that text here in order to illustrate the exercise.

If I was playing John Proctor, I might note that he is:

- Physically strong
- Steady
- Not easily led
- Even tempered
- Honest
- Respected
- Feared
- Lustful
- Ashamed
- Deceitful
- Guilty
- Self-doubting
- Quick to anger
- Conflicted

As you work on the text, you can begin to explore the qualities that you have listed. Start by choosing one of the characteristics from your list. For example, you might approach the scene you are working on through the eyes of a man who is honest and values honesty.

At a given signal, choose another aspect of your character to explore within the same section of text. For example, you could now view the world through the eyes of a man who is experiencing great guilt.

When you again hear the signal, choose a third aspect of the character to play with. For example, you could now choose to focus on the aspect of John Proctor's character that is prone to self-doubt.

Each time you are given the signal, you will jump between the three aspects of character that you have chosen for the exercise. So, if you were working on that exchange between Proctor and Elizabeth, referred to in the previous section, you would have explored it from the viewpoint of a man who is honest, who feels guilty and who suffers from self-doubt.

You can continue to work through the text exploring other qualities from your list. Choose three aspects of character each time to bounce between.

You should approach this exercise playfully and be prepared to take the qualities that you are exploring to extremes. By doing so, you may well see how contradictory some of your character's personality traits are, and how they can fight each other during the dialogue, creating conflict within the character. A character with no conflict in him or her is not dramatically interesting either to watch or for the actor to play.

Through this exercise, you might also discover which qualities the character tries to keep as suppressed inner characteristics, and which manifest themselves outwardly.

Rhythms

Study the scene you are working on and decide what your character's objectives are. Write out your changes of objective as they occur so that you can string them together into a coherent narrative, which will tell the story of the scene from your character's point of view. You will see where the points of highest tension are and how the scene travels either side of these high points.

In order to show you what I mean, let's take the section of the scene between Proctor and Elizabeth from *The Crucible* that we looked at in the previous section. Let's look at it first from Elizabeth's point of view, and then from her husband's.

ELIZABETH. I need you to go to Salem to tell the authorities that Abigail is lying but you are unwilling to do that, which hurts me, and so I need to retreat from you. You tell me now that you were alone with Abigail? This is not what you said before; I need to establish the truth here. You won't give me the truth, so I need to withdraw from you. You tell me to stop being suspicious, but I need to show you that I have reason to be. I need to make you see it from my point of view; I need you to understand that I am not judgemental but that I am justified in the way that I have behaved towards you since I found out what you did with Abigail.

PROCTOR. You want me to go to Salem, but I need to think things over before I accuse Abigail of fraud. I need you to understand why I hesitate to go; no one will believe me anyway as it is just her word against mine. I need you to see that I didn't mention we were alone together, because it was only for a moment and it wasn't at all significant. I need you to stay with me, but I need you to stop doubting me. I have to stop you judging me, to stop our relationship being the way it has been over the past seven months.

When you have written your monologue, read it over to yourself several times until you are familiar with it. Now put the piece of paper down and put on a blindfold, as this will help you to focus on the monologue. The rest of you should also wear blindfolds, or shut your eyes.

This exercise can feel very exposing and there should be no sense that the actor exploring the rhythms is being scrutinised. By shutting down our sight, our hearing is sharpened and any sounds produced will be intensified. Now, without any anticipation, communicate the monologue without words but instead explore the rhythms contained within it. Pay attention to tempo and pace. You can use your breath, beat with your hands on the floor, bang with a chair, tap softly, clap your hands, shuffle your feet; it doesn't matter how you explore the monologue, but do make sure that you have not planned what you are going to do, and that you do not use actual words. Let the rhythm be expressed without censorship as a result of a close reading of the key points that you have noted down.

Take off the blindfold and re-read the monologue. When you are ready, put the blindfold back on, and explore the rhythms again. This time, you will be working with the actors playing the other characters in the scene that you are exploring. One by one, each actor will express the rhythms of their monologues.

When the first actor stops the next begins. Continue to do this repeatedly until you have got a very good sense of each other's rhythms and how they influence your own. See if you can develop a feeling of communication and response between you.

The monologues that you come up with for the scenes that you are working on are likely to be much longer than the examples that I have given you here. I have looked at a section of a scene only.

By exploring the scene in the way that I have outlined, you will get a sense of your character's journey through it, and how it builds and flows. Because you do not 'prepare' for this exercise, all sorts of unpredictable things can happen. Working in this way really means that you embody the rhythms and tempo of your character, and this helps you to gain access to their emotional landscape. It is extraordinary how powerful this work can be: actors often find themselves deeply affected by it as it takes them way out of their comfort zone. It is raw and immediate and connects you directly to your emotions.

By situating different characters' rhythms side by side, you can get a sense of where they come together and where they clash as the scene unfolds. If you look at the little monologues that I have written for Elizabeth and Proctor, you can see clearly what is going on between the two characters. When Mary Warren arrives later in the scene, she will bring in her own rhythms. As you listen to the other characters' rhythms, as well as exploring your own, you will discover all sorts of clashes and discordant notes as well as passages of harmony.

Hot-seating

You should try out this exercise when you have read the play several times and begun working on it as a group.

Write out a character biography listing pivotal facts, experiences, relationships and places that you think have shaped your character. Some information you will gain through a direct reference in the text, but you will also have to use your imagination as you piece together clues in the script which refer obliquely to an experience or fact, or which mention an occurrence that took place before the play begins.

Sit on a chair in front of the rest of the group. You will be introduced to them as your character. They will then ask you questions relating to your life, your relationships, your opinions, etc. For example, they might ask:

- Where do you live?

- How old are you?

- Do you ever get drunk?

- Where did you meet your wife?

- What is your greatest ambition?

- Do you believe in God?

- What keeps you awake at night?

You can choose not to answer a question if you do not feel that it is appropriate for your character to do so.

You can respond to the questioner in any way that you feel fit.

You should find that, as long as you are truly familiar with the play, you can respond to these questions, but there may be questions that you don't know the answer to, as they are not explicitly addressed in the text. These you will answer based on your knowledge of your character's behaviour and predilections. You can be very creative here as long as you can support your answers with something that you have discovered in the text. Remember *how* you answer is as important as *what* you answer, if not more so. What you choose to stay silent about can be more revealing in terms of your character than what you choose to speak out about.

This is not a test to see whether you can list every event in your character's life with accompanying dates! Instead, this is an exercise that can refresh you during the rehearsal process, and remind you of what your character values, fears and reacts to in their life. This exercise can also help you to visualise experiences and so make them more vivid to you when you refer to them in the text.

Fifty Questions

Below is a list of fifty questions that I have thought up for a character in a modern play. You can make your own list that is more relevant to the text that you are working on.

Answer each of the questions from the point of view of your character.

1. What is your full name?

2. How old are you?

3. Have you brothers or sisters?

4. Where were you born?

5. Where did you grow up?

6. Where do you live now?

7. What was school like for you?

8. Who was your best mate at school?

9. What did you want to be when you grew up?

10. What is your job now?

11. Do you like your job?

12. Are you gay or straight?

13. Are you in a relationship?

14. Are you happy in that relationship?

15. What is the worst thing you have ever done?

16. What is the thing that you are proudest of?

17. Who do you love the most in the world?

18. What is your greatest fear?

19. Do you vote? If so, who do you vote for?

20. What music do you listen to?

21. What is your favourite book?

22. What is your favourite film?

23. What is your idea of a perfect day?

24. Do you smoke?

25. Do you take drugs?

26. Do you drink alcohol?

27. What is your favourite drink?

28. Who do you hate most in the world?

29. When or where were you the happiest in your life?

30. What is your favourite item of clothing?

31. Do you play any sports?

32. Do you have any hobbies?

33. What makes you angry?

34. If you could change one thing about yourself, what would it be?

35. What secret about yourself would you least want anyone to know?

36. Have you ever thought about suicide?

37. Do you drive? If so, what do you drive?

38. Do you watch the news?

39. Do you read any newspapers or magazines?

40. What turns you on?

41. What is the landscape you are most comfortable in?

42. What is your favourite season?

43. What is your favourite colour?

44. Do you have any health problems?

45. What do you think about the monarchy?

46. Who is your hero or heroine?

47. Have you ever committed a crime?

48. Who or what was your first love?

49. If you were an animal, what would you be?

50. If you were an element, what would you be: earth, water, air or fire?

Thinking up and answering a list of questions like this can be a useful way of considering your character from different angles. The process should allow you to feel that you have really got to know your character as a three-dimensional being made up of many composite parts, not simply those referred to explicitly in the text. This should give you a sense of confidence, even of security, as you gain a deeper understanding of the things that motivate and influence your character's behaviour. Be careful that you do not answer the questions superficially: there is little point in that. Take time over your answers. Visualise the colours, seasons, etc. Look back over the text repeatedly to gain the information that might lead you to answer the questions as you do. Your answers must be supported by the play and how your character conducts himself within it, so do not be random and unspecific in your responses.

Private Moments

This exercise is useful once you have begun work on the play and are familiar with it.

You are going to explore a moment that your character experiences when they are alone. This moment may be referred to directly in the text, but we do not actually witness it as part of the play itself. The moment you explore can have taken place before the play starts or at any point during it.

Having thought of your moment, you are going to bring in every object that you need to recreate it in the rehearsal room. The moment you are going to explore must be one that involves action for your character, so you cannot simply bring in a duvet and go to sleep under it!

I am going to look at the character of Sonya in Act Two of *Uncle Vanya* by Anton Chekhov as an example. In the play, Sonya invites Doctor Astrov to join her in a midnight feast, telling him that she often treats herself to these little meals. Sonya is very much in love with Astrov, and the experience of spending time alone with him is precious to her. I am going to recreate the midnight feast that Sonya has the following night by herself. This is an event that I have imagined, as we do not see it during the play – indeed, it is not specifically referred to at all.

So that I can recreate the scene physically, I bring in a small chunk of cheese, some bread and some pastries, as well as some juice in a wine bottle. I also bring in two knives, two plates and two glasses. For the table-top, I bring in a cloth and a tiny vase of flowers as well as two candles and matches.

I have written out all the given circumstances around this solitary moment and absorbed them:

Who would I like to be? Astrov's lover and future wife.

Who am I afraid that I am? A plain woman, not attractive enough to be noticed by Astrov in any other capacity than that of a sisterly figure that he is respectful of.

Where am I? In the dining room at home.

When is it? A rainy midnight in late October when everyone else is asleep.

What have I just been doing? The monthly audit for the estate, which took quite some time, as I had no help with it.

What do I want? To eat some food and drink a little wine in peace and quiet, while I remember how I sat at this very table last night with Doctor Astrov. I want to think about all the nights to come when I will sit with him.

What is getting in my way? I know how plain I am and that thought takes away my confidence.

What am I going to do to get what I want? I am going to lay the table beautifully as if he was going to join me. I will light candles and arrange the flowers so they look pretty. I will place the spare plate opposite me and pour a little wine into the spare glass as if he has just put it down having taken a drink. I will sit and taste the food and sip the wine and enjoy this moment, because it reminds me of how we were together last night and allows me to think of the feasts we will share. I can even fantasise that he will return to his place in a moment or two having just gone out to check on the horses.

Having thought out all the given circumstances and brought in everything I need, I will set up my space. I will then engage in my activities, as Sonya, as I have outlined them above. I will lay the table and eat some food in order to explore this moment in the character's life when she is quite alone.

You should allocate about five minutes for each activity that you engage in.

You will explore the exercise in front of the class, but it can also be done alone as part of your private process.

People behave differently when they are alone and unobserved. This exercise allows you to explore how your character behaves within specific circumstances when she is not conscious of being watched, or of having to appear in a certain light. How does she sit? How does she touch the objects around her? How much does her fear of who she might be make itself manifest when at other times it is suppressed?

This exercise should be carefully thought-out and prepared for – but in the doing of it allow yourself to respond to everything around you that happens in that moment. So, in the example of the exercise that I gave you, the candle might go out suddenly, or shine on the wine bottle so that the glass glitters. My back might ache against the chair, a branch may hit the window, I might find myself dancing with excitement at an image that comes to me, or weeping as I remember something from the past. When you are exploring, don't try to force something to happen because you think it should, or because you imagined it that way before you began.

The Power of Music

In relation to the particular scene that you are working on, choose a piece of music that you feel in some way echoes the rhythms, tempo and pace of your character at that point in the text. These elements are fluid and may well alter as the scene develops, but choose something to play with as a starting point for exploration.

Do not rely on lyrics to evoke what is going on for your character. Think about the rhythms, how the music builds or fades, how it reaches a point of explosion or simmers away, never quite finding the release of a crescendo. Think about the mood of the music and its tone. It is unlikely that you will find a piece that reflects everything that is going on for your character at that point, but choose something that you have a strong response to when you listen to it in relation to your character.

Having chosen your piece of music, find a space in the room to listen to it through headphones. Everyone else involved in the scene will be listening to his or her own music at the same time.

When you feel ready, begin to move in response to what the music is doing to you. You can use the whole room or simply occupy a tiny area of it. You can dance, jump, roll or cartwheel! There can be no prescribed way of moving as the music triggers a personal response in you that is not shared by anyone else in the space.

Now locate the person in the scene that you engage with or are most affected by. Continue to listen to the private beat of your own music, but see what happens when you begin to interact with them. Of course they will also be moving to their own rhythms. There will be no words, only your physical expression as you listen to your music. You might find that the rhythms of your own piece complement and seem to work in harmony with the other person, but you may find that you want to retreat from them or square up to them. You cannot predict the outcome of the meeting. You will now be affected by your own music, but also by how your partner is responding to you as a result of listening to theirs. There is no need to synchronise this in any way; it is not a dance and so needs no choreography.

Now, one pair at a time works, while the rest of the class observes. Stand opposite each other and remove the headphones from one ear so that each of you is listening to music through one ear only. Begin to play the scene, either speaking the text or improvising it using your own words. Your music will still affect you, but you will also be able to hear what is being said to you.

As the scene progresses, each of you removes the second headphone so that you can no longer hear your music. Focus simply on the other character, but allow whatever you felt as a result of that music to inform the interaction.

We all know how evocative music is. A particular track can trigger vivid memories of people and places, a time of life, of smells even. Music can bypass our rational minds and get right to the centre of our emotional core, and because of this it is a very useful tool. When you get caught up in your head trying to work through something logically, listening to music can key in to basic urges and responses and bring you back into your body.

This exercise is particularly useful, not only because it helps you to connect emotionally, but also because it gives you access to the rhythms of the scene. Through it, you can get a further sense of where there is conflict between characters, and where there is resolve.

When we talk about character, it is possible to have a notion of a fixed identity, of a person who behaves in the way they do because it is inherent in their nature to do so. I think that human beings are far more complex and fluid creatures than such a notion allows for, so these exercises should assist you in looking for possible characteristics and qualities that your character may have that influence them, but they should not steer you away from the idea that the circumstances often dictate how a person behaves. Perhaps in different circumstances, Hamlet would have killed Claudius in Act One!

As a result of this work you should:

- Be able to explore conflicting aspects within your character.

- Access aspects of your character's emotional life through rhythm.

- Be able to ask relevant questions and answer them in a way that offers you a deeper understanding of your character's life.

- Understand the power of music as a tool for accessing emotion and probing the shifts within a character and the conflicts between characters.

- Be able to explore your character outside of the constraints of the text, but informed by a detailed reading of that text.

Written Work

Although the vast majority of the work that you will do at a drama school is practical – acting is, after all, a vocation and a craft – it is also likely that you will be required to submit some written work. At the time of writing there are twenty-one drama schools represented by Drama UK (the organisation promoting vocational and professional drama training in the UK; www.dramauk.co.uk), out of which eighteen offer degree courses in acting, the majority of which are Honours degrees. It is little wonder then that you may be called upon to do some writing as an element of your training. Although it is only one area of written work, this section will focus specifically on offering you advice for writing essays, as students are often particularly daunted by this element of their course.

For some of you this won't be a problem, but for others it might. You have, after all, signed up to train on a practical course, and you may feel that writing is not one of your strong points. It is, however, a component, relatively small in the case of drama schools, of gaining a degree – and it could be argued that it is a really useful thing that actors now come away from their training, not only equipped to meet the demands of the acting industry, but also armed with a qualification that can help them to secure other types of work when acting jobs are thin on the ground. At some point you might also want to study at a higher level or narrow your specialism, and a degree paves the way for you to do that.

Perhaps, even more importantly, you could view the writing process in a positive light as an end in itself, and by doing so understand why its practice has been included on your course. Through written work:

- You can focus and organise your thoughts.

- You can reflect on your process.

- You can evaluate different ideas and methodologies in a clear and tangible way.

- You can identify moments of inspiration or understanding, and record them to remind yourself of them at a later date.

- You can develop your own point of view and chart your thinking as it expands.

- You can even enjoy writing as a creative outlet!

So, if you try and see writing as a positive element of your training, you will probably find it easier to engage with the written tasks you may be set, even if you struggle in the process. You have been selected on to an acting programme because of your acting skills, so no one is expecting you to be a masterful writer as well. I teach a lot of very intelligent people, some of whom find ordering their thoughts on paper easy, and some of whom do not. Quite a number of the students that I meet are dyslexic, for example, or quite simply lack confidence after years at school being told that their written work is inadequate. There will be appropriate support to help you with written assignments at drama school, but the secret is not to panic. The emphasis is on your thinking, on your perception, on your developing process, not on how wonderfully you communicate it all on paper. Writing is just one form of recording ideas, and you may find that you discover all sorts of other ways of doing so alongside it.

Here are some examples of the type of written tasks, as well as essays, that you might be set at drama school:

- You may be asked to write your own monologues, as we have seen during some of the exercises outlined in previous sections – for example, during the work exploring rhythm.

- You may be asked to write a character biography, like the one asked of the actors in preparation for the 'Hot-seating' exercise.

- You may be asked to keep some sort of record of your learning, a reflective journal perhaps, which traces your work over the course of your training and requires some written observations.

- You may be asked to submit a final-year research project that has a written component to it.

- You may be asked to write essays as a means of reflecting on and evaluating your process, and the methodologies and ideas that you come into contact with.

Writing Your Essay

a. Before you start your essay, make sure that you feel confident in exactly what is being asked of you. How long should it be? How should it be presented? How have you been told to reference it? Make sure that you read the essay title several times so that you really understand it. Make sure you know what the title is asking of you, what does it want you to think about?

b. Make sure that you understand the key words involved in the title. Some common words are:

Define – Write the precise meaning of the word or phrase or idea. There may be more than one definition available.

Compare – Look at the similarities and differences. You may be asked to judge between them.

Explain – Illustrate, account for. Give reasons why.

Describe – Give a detailed account of.

Evaluate – Consider the worth of something, whether it is useful or achieves its aims, has some merit. You will need to give evidence for your appraisal of its value.

Contrast – Consider the differences.

Criticise – Give your judgement about how successful the theories are. You must support this with evidence for your reasoning.

Discuss – Look at the arguments, set up a debate between them.

c. It is sometimes hard to know where to begin with research. There is so much available both on the internet and from other sources that you can easily become overwhelmed. Go back to the question again and nail down exactly what is being asked. Write a list of the key points and questions that come to you when you re-read the question. Use these initial thoughts as a starting point from which to begin your research. As well as using the internet, refer to magazines, newspapers, papers written by academics on the subject, TV programmes, radio, your notes from classes and, of course, books. A librarian will be able to point you in the right direction so that you can find what you need.

d. You need to be able to order the research that you do, so you must *plan* your essay. With this in mind, start as soon as you are given the title so as to allow yourself sufficient time to do this – if you leave it till the last moment you will not. Planning gives you a basic structure from which to work, and this scaffold will help you to feel more confident. By drawing up a plan you can see what the key ideas behind the essay are, which will prevent you from going off on tangents or leaving something vital out. The skeleton of your plan should be: *Introduction > Main body of essay > Conclusion*. In the *introduction*, you should explain what you understand by the essay title, define any terms that you need to and set out the aims of the essay, giving the readers a clear idea of what to expect. Be concise and to the point here. In the *main body* of the essay you will flesh out everything you outlined in the introduction with detail, examples and discussion, all supported by evidence coming from your research. In the *conclusion*, you will summarise the main ideas. You might evaluate your findings and bring in your own opinions – as long as these are supported by those findings. It may be appropriate to point out where further research might go in the future as a way of approaching the problem.

Example:
If I was approaching the essay title: 'With reference to the methodologies you have encountered during your studies, give a detailed account of how you would go about preparing for a role as one of the characters from *The Crucible*.' This is how I might go about things:

Introduction – I need to *understand* and *define* the aims of the task, so firstly I will consider concisely what is meant by 'methodology' in this context; that is the ideas that have been explored during acting classes. I will outline the key methodologies that I will be considering in the essay – for example, exercises deriving from Stanislavsky's system and Meisner's ideas about acting being 'the reality of doing'. I will state briefly why I have chosen these particular methodologies and anticipate any outcome that I think that the essay will arrive at. I will say what character I have chosen to look at, and why.

Main body – Now I need to get on with it. I will *consider* in detail the methodologies that I have selected and the ideas behind them that might help me to realise the role. I will *compare* and *contrast* methodologies. For example, I might look at Meisner's emphasis on imagination in contrast to ideas about emotional memory. I might consider the revisiting of events that have actually happened in my life, which Stanislavsky explored for a time, and which Lee Strasberg, the founder of the school of 'Method Acting', valued. I will *discuss* how I would use the ideas in preparation for my role, and why and when they would be useful.

Conclusion – I will *summarise* the whole process concisely and *evaluate* my choices in relation to the role. I will *criticise* any of the choices that I found were not as useful having thought about them in this context, and I will consider how I might develop the work in the future.

e. Try writing a first draft that follows your plan and gets all your ideas down so that you can see whether you are covering the points that you want to.

f. When you write your final draft, use simple, straightforward language, avoiding slang and abbreviations. Shorter sentences tend to be easier to read. Make sure that there is no padding with irrelevant information and rambling ideas. The reader wants to follow the argument; they don't need to be impressed by your clever use of language or by the fact that you have included lots of extra facts, whether or not they are relevant. Try to link the paragraphs so that the thoughts contained in each one follow on from each other, making it easy to read. A paragraph normally deals with one topic, issue or idea. Two paragraphs might be on different topics but linked by their differences or similarities.

Some good 'linking' phrases are:

To contrast: however / on the other hand / but

To explain: for example / for instance

Taking the argument further: similarly / furthermore / in addition

Concluding: therefore / as a result / consequently

g. Look back over the essay and ask yourself the following questions:

- Have I answered the question?

- Have I covered the main points that I set out to?

- Have I covered them in enough detail?

- Have I supported my argument with examples and references?

- Have I distinguished clearly between what are my own thoughts and what belong to others?

- Have I acknowledged all the sources that influenced the argument, and have I referenced any quotes that I have used or ideas that I have found?

- Are the paragraphs ordered clearly so that the argument is easy to read?

- Have I used clear language?

- Have I used the correct punctuation, grammar and spelling?

- Is the essay the right length?

- Have I included a list at the end of the essay detailing any books, websites or other materials that I have used for my research?

I hope that this offers you a helpful guide. There will be plenty of support available at your college, so there is no need to be anxious at the prospect of writing essays. It is unlikely that there will be a great deal of essay-writing, but if you can engage with the purpose of it, realise how writing an essay might actually serve you by helping you to collect and distil your thoughts, understand your process and be able to contextualise it, then perhaps you may not find this element of your training such a chore!

Through this process, you should:

- Be able to organise your thoughts.

- Be able to use appropriate language to further your argument.

- Be able to offer definitions of any terms that you use.

- Be able to structure an argument so that you introduce the ideas, lead us through the thoughts and summarise the arguments in a conclusion.

- See the purpose behind the written element of your course rather than view it simply as a chore.

Part Two
Second Year:
Beyond the Self

Beyond the Self

If your training is working for you, then you should enter the second year not only armed with tools to help you approach the work, but also from a position of greater confidence than when you began your course. Now you are about to embark on the next chapter of your training, but before you go on to look at the exercises outlined in the following pages, it is important that you understand something fundamental: the work that you have done to release you, to open you, to ignite your imaginations and allow access to your emotional resources should never leave you. You should always work responsively, you should always be specific and active in your choices, and you should always be open to the demands of the project.

Many of the exercises outlined in Part One will be applied to the texts that you are likely to come across in the second year of your training; they do not become irrelevant because the nature of the plays you are working on might change. It may be that you choose to ignore some exercises and adapt others, but the foundation that the first year provides you with, as an actor, should remain firm as you continue to use and develop the tools that it offered you.

I am reminding you of this because I have seen actors become almost schizophrenic as they take on the challenges of the second year. As they begin to work on texts that are less naturalistic than they are used to, they split themselves in two: one part of them is instinctive and emotionally responsive, and the other is intellectually active and technical. Joining these elements up lies at the heart of your training. A good actor is responsive, open and alive to the moment, but needs also to have technique and control as well as an understanding of the wider implications of the text.

Although some students initially feel constricted by the demands made on them by texts that are not naturalistic, feeling unable to use the spontaneous and responsive approach that they had found in the first year, some are liberated by the opportunity to explore other forms of expression. Either way, the training that you experience in your second year should follow on from previous ideas, as well as extend and expand your thinking. Part Two does not necessarily provide you with any solutions; rather it attempts to show you some of the questions that will arise as you continue your exploration of different texts. It will give you a sense of some of the issues that may confront you, and even confuse you, as you enter your second year of drama-school training.

Extending Naturalism

You should have more strength both physically and vocally now that you have undergone a year of training. Many of the texts that you will look at during your second year will require this increase of strength. You will also be expected to work more independently than perhaps you did previously, as you begin to take increased responsibility for reflecting on and developing your own process. You will now be working on a range of texts written in different styles and which may have at their heart a political, social or ideological focus. In the first year, to a large extent, you concentrated on plays that required you to understand your character psychologically; the texts of the second year may ask you, in addition, to consider context, style, genre and the aesthetic demands of the production. You will be encouraged to make choices that are informed by some or all of these elements. It is likely too that you will begin to work with heightened language. The next section will look specifically at Shakespeare, but you will come across plenty of other playwrights whose language is complex or poetic. You will also be challenged to consider the relationship between the actor and the audience, and to investigate ways of addressing that audience. You may be asked to play with stylised forms of presentation and so extend from a truthful inner life to explore a wider picture of the world and its politics. Initially, you may find yourself pushed well outside the boundaries of your comfort zone.

Aims

- To explain in more detail the demands of the
  second year that vary from the first year.

- To outline the traditions that some of the texts that you will be working on come from.

- To encourage you to question your role as an actor, and to consider the demands of different texts that you will be working on.

- To offer you a practical way of understanding different approaches.

- To look at ways of fusing the physical expression of an attitude with a rich inner life.

- To offer ways of demystifying complex argument.

- To encourage you to view yourself as a storyteller, an activist who can provoke thought in your audience as well as feelings.

The Nature of the Texts

During the first year, you focused on texts that required you to engage with a role by paying very close attention to detail based on observation of real life. You considered the psychological motivation of the character, and you were aware of the given circumstances that surrounded the choices that your character made. Many of the texts that you will encounter in the second year come from European theatre traditions that challenge this naturalistic way of working. There are lots of books, papers and websites available for you to research further, but it will be useful for me to outline very broadly a few of the ideas contained within some of the traditions, so that you will be able to contextualise and understand better the exercises that follow. These explanations are intended to provide you with only a general sense of the texts that you will be exploring; you will need to research in far more detail for yourself in order to understand them in any depth. I have listed some of the writers associated with each tradition so that you can read their work and get a sense of the plays. Notice where they differ from the more naturalistic texts that you might have been used to, and also where a naturalistic style of acting might nonetheless be appropriate within them. Notice where the demands made on the actor requires him or her to combine a physical embodiment of an attitude with a really rich inner life.

Epic Theatre

Bertolt Brecht, the German poet, playwright and director so influential in the twentieth century, proposed that a play should not cause an audience to lose themselves emotionally in the experiences of the characters onstage. Those watching should not be swept away by feelings but should be provoked instead to engage in a process of rational self-reflection, and to respond critically to what they are seeing. He wanted the audience to watch his plays and then to leave the theatre intent on making a change in the world outside. Epic theatre for Brecht was a forum for political ideas. By reminding the audience that a play is something that is created, an attempt is made to show that, just as events onstage can be changed, so too can those in real life.

In order to illuminate the constructed nature of a play, techniques are used to remind those watching that a play is a *representation* of reality and not reality itself. So, for example, characters address the audience directly, they sing songs to break up and comment on the action, plac-ards may be produced to offer further information about the onstage action. The actor is required to extend the psychological approach, and to shape their character both in terms of their actions and their physicality in order to show the political argument of the play.

Apart from Brecht, other examples of playwrights you might come across from this tradition include Peter Weiss and Edward Bond. Many current writers (e.g. Simon Stephens) use Brechtian technique as one of several devices in their plays.

Absurdist Theatre

Playwrights within this tradition expressed the idea that our universe is without a god, and because of this, human beings live pretty meaningless existences. Living in a godless universe implies that there is no rationale behind life. There was no plan for or purpose to our existence, and so logical and rational ways of dealing with the world and each other break down. The world is losing (or has lost) its sense of reason, and the actor is required to support this vision of a strange landscape where speech is often illogical and irrational, though frequently poetic. This will make great demands on you to find appropriate physical and vocal expression. You will be required to contribute to the rhythmic and visual representations of such a world.

Playwrights you may come across here include Samuel Beckett, Jean Genet, Harold Pinter, Tom Stoppard, Edward Albee and Eugène Ionesco.

Expressionist Theatre

Expressionist theatre aims to evoke moods and ideas and to offer an emotional experience to the audience, rather than to present a naturalistic reality. It uses exaggeration and distortion as it attempts to show an essence of life, to look at the meaning of being alive itself, not simply to mimic something from the real world. It often deals with spiritual awakenings and suffering for its protagonists, and the characters are frequently simplified, based on mythic types. Choral effects are often used.

The actor must engage with heightened, stylised, poetic language, and this will require you to extend physically and vocally, and to be able to sustain this extension.

Playwrights you may come across here include Federico García Lorca, Ferdinand Bruckner, Ernst Toller, Frank Wedekind and Nikolai Gogol.

Theatre of Catastrophe

Howard Barker coined this term to describe his work, because his characters function so often in a state of crisis, at a time of social breakdown. His plays often explore the desire for power, sex and violence, basic motivations that drive human beings. He doesn't want the audience to have a collective response to what they are viewing onstage; instead he wants those watching to understand the play from the perspective of the individual. He doesn't try to make scenes clear, but works to make them more ambiguous, thereby giving the individual audience member more to struggle with. The motivations of his characters are often hard to nail down, as contradictions and paradoxes emerge in their behaviour and desires. The actor who is used to mapping out the motivations of his character psychologically – tracing one moment from another in a logical sequence resulting in a particular behaviour or action – will struggle here. You will need to find a way of extending that psychological approach and also of working with language that can at times be extremely complex.

Some other texts that you will work on will contain elements of more than one of these traditions – for example, some of the work of Edward Bond or Caryl Churchill.

Ancient Greek Tragedy

It is important to remember that, although these plays originated from an ancient culture quite remote from your own, they are endlessly open to interpretation and able to adapt and respond to the needs of a modern audience. Two thousand years before Shakespeare, the oldest surviving form of tragedy emerged, and from it all Western theatre has originated. Tragedies were usually based on traditional legends in a world controlled by the gods of Greek mythology. The main characters were noble, while the chorus – who could comment on the action, but were powerless to intervene in it – comprised of women, slaves and old men. The entire cast was exclusively male, made up of no more than three actors accompanied by twelve to fifteen chorus members. Masks that covered the entire head were worn, as were elaborate costumes. The stakes in these plays are always high. Themes reflect the vulnerability of human life and the often inescapable consequences of the decisions that humans make. They are concerned with how the protagonists respond to their misfortunes. They essentially deal with drama between humans, rather than between humans and gods.

The plays would have been written for a one-off performance, and played to a huge audience in the open air. They would begin with a prologue, which was either a monologue or dialogue, but which provided information about the setting and the initial situation. The chorus then identified themselves before the drama began. Scenes were alternated with songs sung by the chorus, who finally concluded the action with a few sung lines. The actors mainly used spoken verse, while the chorus sang and danced.

Playwrights you may come across are Aeschylus, Sophocles and Euripides.

A Different Approach

Two of you come into the space while the rest of the group watches.

Sit on chairs facing each other. Decide which one of you will be the doctor, and which will be the patient. You will be given this script to read from:

DOCTOR. We have your test results back. They
    show that the cancer is benign but you will
    need to come back in a month. You should
    book an appointment at reception.

PATIENT. Thank you, doctor.

After you have read the lines through a couple of times, you should memorise them and play the scene without referring to the script. It is very short so that should be easily achievable. You should use whatever clues that you can glean from the text in order to communicate the story of this short exchange. The patient, for instance, knows that he is there to find out if he has cancer or not, and the doctor knows that the tumour is benign.

A big sheet of paper is tacked on to the wall behind you with this information written on it: 'This Doctor Does Not Respect This Patient Because He Does Not Pay for the Treatment.' Everyone watching is able to see this statement.

You should now play the scene again – however, none of what is written on the sheet of paper should be evident in your performance. The information written on that sheet provides those watching with the facts required in order to read what they need into the performance, without you having to do anything but deliver the lines. In this way, the audience is given a clear insight into the social hierarchy inherent in the scene that they are witnessing.

Now play the scene again, but this time you must provide your audience with the same information but without the help of that useful sheet of paper behind you. How are you going to do that?

As you go through a process of self-direction in order to achieve the aim of the scene, you should consider various things – for example, body language. Should the doctor sit while the patient stands or vice versa? Does the doctor make eye contact or perhaps look out of the window throughout? Does the doctor keep shooting glances at her watch? What is the rhythm of delivery? Does the doctor speak slowly because she is bored? Or does she speed up when she sees what the time is? Does she fiddle with a file on the desk, or toy with the phone? You might like to ask yourself where the doctor would rather be at this time? Perhaps she is tired and at some point stretches surreptitiously. During all this, what is the patient doing? These are simply some ideas to start you off. You should continue to explore until you are satisfied that you have communicated the information that was written on the paper in a clear and engaging way for your audience.

This exercise comes from work developed by director David Zoob. It serves a simple but useful function in that it demonstrates how the actor may, within the context of particular texts, make choices that are not based on motivation but on making sure a point is made to the audience. You still need to fill these choices with inner life, but as a starting point you can play with a physical articulation of the scene, not only a psychological one. In order to make these physical choices, however, you need to think about the political attitude of both the play and the character.

Another useful idea that this exercise introduces is that of '*gestus*', which can be interpreted as a physical embodiment of an attitude. It is a term that you may have come across before. During the little scene that you considered in the exercise, I offered you the idea that the doctor might stretch surreptitiously. In this context, the stretch is a physical action that shows very clearly a disrespectful attitude towards her patient. Here is an example of *gestus* and it serves to inform the audience of the same message that had previously been visible on the piece of paper.

This exercise is simply a practical way of getting you to consider that there are different ways of approaching and delivering text; it offers an alternative starting point.

Making the Text More Concrete

Look at the following short speech from the play *The Homecoming* by Harold Pinter. Lenny is talking about the problem he has with the logic of Christian theism, which argues that God cannot be known:

LENNY. Well look at it this way. How can the unknown merit reverence? In other words, how can you revere that of which you are ignorant? At the same time, it would be ridiculous to propose that what we *know* merits reverence. What we know merits any one of a number of things, but it stands to reason reverence isn't one of them. In other words, apart from the known and the unknown, what else is there?

Underline any word or phrase that you think is of particular significance in the speech, in terms of the argument. For example:

LENNY. Well look at it this way. How can the <u>unknown</u> merit <u>reverence</u>? In other words, <u>how can you revere that of which you're ignorant</u>? At the same time, it would be <u>ridiculous</u> to propose that what we <u>*know*</u> merits <u>reverence</u>. What we know merits <u>any one of a number of things</u>, but it stands to <u>reason</u> reverence isn't one of them. In other words, <u>apart from the known and the unknown, what else is there</u>?

Having gone through the speech in this way, get a large sheet of paper and do a drawing on it of everything that you have underlined. You may write words as part of this drawing, but these must only come from the text itself. The images that you draw are personal to you, as this exercise is done individually and not collectively as a group. You don't need to draw the ideas in a logical, linear way; you can arrange them as you like on the paper rather than make a comic-strip presentation of them. You should be trying to draw the essence of the ideas rather than a sequential representation of them. It doesn't matter if you're not very good at drawing; the idea is to negotiate your way through the speech in order to get a concrete understanding of what is going on in it. Abstract concepts can be made specific to you by what you choose to draw in relation to them.

In this speech, Lenny is arguing that it is pointless worshipping something that cannot be known – if you cannot know God, how can you revere God? On the other hand, why would you worship something that you do know, because nothing that we know really deserves that level of reverence? So, if it is unreasonable to worship either the unknown or the known, what is there left to worship? These are tricky ideas; what will you draw for 'unknown'? What does what you 'know' look like? What are these 'number of things' that the character refers to?

Stick your picture on the wall, and this time as you go through the speech touch the images each time you come to the word or concept that they illustrate. As you do so, be aware of how you make contact with everything that you have drawn. For example, do you stroke the image? Do you flick it? Do you slap it? How does the way you touch the drawing affect the delivery of the speech? The process of delivering the speech as you make contact with the corresponding images allows you to make a physical connection to the words as you speak them.

Repeat this, but this time as if you are a university lecturer. Deliver the speech to the rest of the group. Speak the words and touch the images for the benefit of the group, who need to understand the ideas within it.

Finally, do the speech to the rest of the group again, but this time without referring at all to the picture. You should be able to connect to the ideas but also to open the speech out and share it with your audience.

This exercise aims to demystify text, and to turn the abstract into something more concrete; to lift it out of the intellect so that the speech becomes something far more tangible and visceral for you to play with. You can apply it to any bit of text that is complex and tricky to get inside of. It will be a useful exercise to return to when you do Shakespeare.

This is not a free-association exercise in which a word will trigger all sorts of apparently unrelated images from your own life. Draw only what is mentioned in the speech. Do not lose sight of the argument. In this way, although the images are personal, they also serve to illuminate the specific point that the writer is trying to make. The idea behind communicating the speech to the rest of the group as if it was a lecture supports this – you are opening the speech up, not just for yourself but also for the benefit of an audience.

Points of Concentration

For this exercise, we will return to *The Cherry Orchard* by Anton Chekhov. Notice that we are returning to a text that could be described as naturalistic.

Think about the following incident, which takes place towards the end of Act Two:

They all remain seated, deep in thought. The only sound is that of old FIRS, *muttering as usual. Suddenly a far-off noise is heard, as if in the heavens – like the sound of a breaking string, dying away, sadly.*

Ask yourselves these questions:

a. What does that sound of the breaking string signify? (Think about the other time you hear the same sound in the play. Firs also refers to it happening at a specific time in the past.)

b. What does an actor have to do to convey this meaning? (Should the actor simply play their actions, connect to the emotional truth, and leave the rest to the director?)

c. What does the sound of the string breaking mean to each of the characters? Look at how they react to the event:

RANEVSKAYA. What was that?

LOPAKHIN. I don't know. Possibly a coal-tub broken loose somewhere, down the mines. A long way from here, anyway.

GAEV. Could be some sort of bird, like a heron.

TROFIMOV. Or an owl, perhaps....

RANEVSKAYA (*shudders*). It's horrible, whatever it is.

A pause.

FIRS. It was the same before the disaster. The owl started screeching, and the samovar wouldn't stop buzzing.

GAEV. Before what disaster?

FIRS. Before the Freedom.

A pause.

RANEVSKAYA. Well, anyway, let's go in, it's getting late. Anya dear, you're crying... what's the matter?

Embraces her.

ANYA. It's all right, Mama, it's nothing.

Notice that Varya, another important character who is present, doesn't speak about the sound at all.

Cast the scene and read it through. Mark the sound of the string breaking by reading the stage directions that describe it.

Now, using each person's response as a point of concentration, read through those stage directions again. A point of concentration simply means whatever it is that you, as the character, are concentrating on at that moment. So go over the section and focus on each of the character's responses in turn, one after the other, as they hear the sound of the breaking string. Even though she doesn't speak, concentrate on Varya's response to it too. Focus specifically on each character's *distinct* response. For example, which characters are frightened? Which characters are intrigued? Which characters are exhilarated?

Having looked at each character in turn, now put all the reactions together, and this time work as a group to create a choreographed composite of all the responses. Spend time really exploring the reactions physically. Those watching should be able to see whether the significance of the moment is revealed through this extended focus on the attitudes towards the event, and to direct those onstage as to how to make the moment clearer if they need to do so.

For example, Lopakhin's response is practical: he is industrious and he links the sound to industry. How might he stand? What gesture or gestures might you come up with in relation to his pragmatism? If he were an element – earth, fire, air, water – which would he be? How could you express that? How would he relate to the other characters physically, in the immediate aftermath of that haunting sound?

This exercise sets out to make you question your role as an actor. It does not seek to provide any answers to that question, but you should be provoked by it to consider to what extent your knowledge of the greater significance of a moment informs you as an actor. Should you think thematically or conceptually? Does doing so assist your acting? If you feel that the sound of the breaking string serves as a reminder of the rapid passage of time heralding huge social changes and the death of the old order, what impact, if any, does this have on your playing of that moment?

Isolating points of concentration is a very useful way of distilling what is happening at that moment onstage. This can help you to understand what your own character is focusing on, but it can also help you to communicate an idea to the audience, whose attention can be guided to a particular image or reaction.

All this talk of concepts and themes can cause you to over-intellectualise and lose the dynamic of the action. By expressing yourself physically, and extending that expression, you may well find that you feel liberated again. Ideas originate in the head, but they can only really communicate themselves onstage when they are located in the body. Heightening your physical reaction to an event can remind you of this, and also connect you to something tangible and therefore easier to fully understand.

Uniting by Subject Change

Take a speech that you are currently working on and mark the text each time that the subject changes.

I will give you an example using part of Lopakhin's big speech from Act Three of *The Cherry Orchard*. I have put a forward slash to mark each change of subject.

LOPAKHIN. I bought it! Ladies and gentlemen, please, wait – I've a bit of a thick head, I can't speak... (*Laughs.*) When we got to the auction, Deriganov was already there. Leonid Andreyich had only fifteen thousand, and straight away Deriganov bid another thirty, on top of the mortgage. Well, I could see how things were going, so I waded in with forty thousand. He went up to forty-five, so I bid fifty-five. He would go up by five, you see, and I'd bid another ten. Well, it finished eventually. I bid ninety thousand roubles over and above the mortgage, and it was knocked down to me. The cherry orchard's mine now. All mine! (*Laughs.*) Tell me I'm drunk, or crazy, tell me I'm imagining all this … / (*Stamps his feet.*) No, don't laugh at me! / If only my father and grandfather could rise up out of their graves, and see all that's happened – how their little Yermolai, their abused, semi-literate Yermolai, who used to run around barefoot in winter – how that same Yermolai has bought this estate, the most beautiful spot on earth. / Yes, I've bought the land on which my father and grandfather were slaves, where they weren't even allowed into the kitchen. I must be asleep, it's all just a dream, it's all in the mind… It's your imagination at work, shrouded in mystery… / (*Picks up the keys, smiling affectionately.*) She threw down the keys, to show she's no longer mistress of this house. (*Jingles the keys.*) Well, it doesn't matter. /

The musicians are heard tuning up.

Hey, musicians, let's hear you play! / Come on in, all of you, and watch Yermolai Lopakhin take his axe to the cherry orchard, see the trees falling down! We're going to build cottages here, and our grandsons and great-grandsons'll see a whole new life… / Come on, let's have some music!

The orchestra starts playing. / RANEVSKAYA *slumps into a chair, weeping bitterly.*

> LOPAKHIN *reproaches her.*
>
> Why didn't you listen to me, eh? Why not? Oh, my poor dear lady, there's no going back now. (*A catch in his voice.*) / God, I wish all this was over and done with, I wish our miserable, disjointed lives could be somehow changed.

In the earlier section 'Working with Text', you explored ways of breaking down the script so that it was divided up into manageable chunks to work on. These divisions were decided by a change of objective for the characters involved in the scene. The text was arranged into units, and the process of dividing the text up in this way is called uniting. In this exercise, you are also being asked to divide the text up into units, but this time they are decided by a subject change in the speech, and not necessarily by a change of objective. It may well be that you would mark different sections of the text to indicate a change of subject, but I simply wanted to show you another way of clarifying the thoughts within a speech, enabling you to see the path of the narrative more clearly. There will be overlaps between uniting in this way and uniting with objectives because they aren't always distinct from each other. Marking the subject shifts allows you to view the speech objectively, to get a sense of the whole. It is useful when the thoughts are very complex or when the character is drunk or in shock or spinning with emotion in some way, as Lopakhin is during this extraordinary speech.

Clarifying the Subject Changes Further

You will need a stack of paper cups and different coloured pens.

Having marked your speech for changes of subject as you did in the previous exercise, write a title for each subject on the base of a cup, with one title per cup, and each written in a different colour. You can choose whatever title is meaningful and specific to you. Don't write the same title on more than one cup, even if it is returned to during the speech.

Using Lopakhin's speech from Act Three of *The Cherry Orchard* again, I will give you an example of what I mean. These are the titles that I would write on the bases of the cups:

- Triumph at the auction.

- Don't mock me.

- Abused Yermolai wins.

- Descended from slaves.

- Varya gives up power.

- Party music.

- Old trees for new cottages.

- Ranevskaya's pain.

- Miserable lives.

Place the cups around the space that you are working in with the base visible so that you can see what is written there.

As you go through the speech aloud, pick up the cup that corresponds to whatever it is that you are talking about.

When you are no longer talking about that particular thing, then put the cup back down. If you are talking about more than one thing at once you may keep hold of as many of the cups as you need.

This is a very simple exercise that you can use when you need to pinpoint exactly what it is that you are talking about at any time. It helps to clarify a speech, and to make sure that you understand what the character is dealing with during it. With some speeches you will find yourself juggling more than one cup, and sometimes you will find that there is one cup that you keep coming back to or have difficulty letting go of, even when it appears that you are talking about something else. This should give you further insight into how your character's thoughts travel through the speech, fastening on to different subjects.

From One Extreme to Another

Take two emotional extremes, for example agony and ecstasy.

Imagine that one end of the room represents one of the extremes, and the opposite end represents the other. You could write each state on a piece of paper and stick it to the appropriate wall if you need reminding.

Place chairs between the states of emotion that you have designated for each end of the room. Each chair represents a gradation towards or away from either state; so make sure that there are plenty of them. It doesn't matter if you have too many, that is better than not having enough.

Think where your character is emotionally at the beginning of the scene or speech. In terms of where they are in relation to the two states you have chosen, sit on an appropriate chair. Each time there is a shift in the emotion towards one or other of the states you must move to another chair. You can think about the line as you are travelling between chairs, but you can only speak it out loud when you are actually sitting down.

Go through the entire scene or speech in this way. You may well find yourself running to a particular chair as the drive towards or away from the particular emotion becomes intensified.

Good texts to work on to explore this exercise are Eugène Ionesco's *The Bald Prima Donna*, and Harold Pinter's *The Lover*, but there are many others for which it would be appropriate.

This exercise follows on from the simpler exercise, 'Changing Chairs', where you are asked to move to a new chair each time you have a shift in objective. The purpose of that exercise was to enable you to 'score' a text, in order to understand the thought processes and shifts of direction within it. The exercise above serves the same function in that it helps you to make sense of the text in a dynamic and active way. It is particularly useful when you are working on farce, where the characters tend to move from one extreme to another very quickly.

Agony and ecstasy are good emotional states to pick, although you might find alternatives depending on what you are working on and wish to look at within it. The exercise encourages you to explore and commit to extreme states of emotion instinctively; it is not something that you map out before you start. This way of working brings the text to life as it pushes you to embody the emotional shift as you move, but it also allows you to be very precise as each of these shifts are scored in the text.

Those involved in the particular scene you are working on should do the exercise while the rest of the group observes.

Combining the Private with the Public

For an example of the sort of text that this exercise might be particularly useful for, look at the following exchange between the ruler Creon and his son Haemon from Sophocles' *Antigone*. (I am using Marianne McDonald's translation, published by Nick Hern Books.) Creon has condemned his son's fiancée, Antigone, to death, after she has explicitly gone against his ruling and buried her brother. Haemon, Creon's son, has come to talk with his father. The dialogue below has been preceded by speeches from each man offering their side of the argument. The chorus is present throughout, witnessing and commenting on the action. Haemon will go on to kill himself over Antigone's body.

CREON. So, am I, leader of the city, in my mature years, in full possession of all my powers, to be taught by an immature boy like you?

HAEMON. Only if I'm right; consider what I say, not my age.

CREON. Are you saying we should accept anarchy?

HAEMON. No!

CREON. But can't you see that that's what she is doing, breeding anarchy.

HAEMON. The people of our city don't think so.

CREON. Now it's the city that tells me how I should rule?

HAEMON. Father, you're behaving like a child. No city belongs to one man.

CREON. Doesn't the city's authority come from its ruler?

HAEMON. You're not ruling a desert, father, but a city full of people.

CREON (to CHORUS). She's poisoned his mind against me.

HAEMON. No; I'm on your side.

CREON. Aren't you ashamed to stand there and question your father in front of others?

HAEMON. Not when I see him acting unfairly.

CREON. What is unfair about respecting and discharging the responsibilities of my office?

HAEMON. But you show no respect – you trample on the gods!

CREON. And you trample on filial piety! You are worse than a woman!

HAEMON. I'm not ashamed of what I've said, Father.

CREON. You can't stop pleading her case, can you!

HAEMON. I am pleading for you too, for me, and for the gods below.

CREON. She will not live to marry you!

HAEMON. If she dies she'll take someone else with her.

CREON. So now you have the gall to threaten me!

HAEMON. There is no threat in telling you the truth.

CREON. You'll be sorry for this. You don't understand anything.

HAEMON. If you were not my father, I would say that you had lost your senses.

CREON. You're completely in her power! Stop wasting my time!

HAEMON. Won't you listen to a thing I'm saying?

CREON. I've had enough! By God, I'm not going to stand here and let you insult me a moment longer! I'll teach you! Drag out that viper, so she can die here on the spot, next to her bridegroom.

HAEMON. I'll never let that happen. She won't die next to me. I'm leaving. Do your worst, Father. You will never see me again.

Exit HAEMON.

Read through your scene with a partner, one of you taking on the role of Creon, the other of his son

Haemon. Make sure that you understand the text in terms of its meaning.

Each man is presenting an argument. Play the scene as if it is taking place in a courtroom where a jury must decide who is in the right and who is not. The debate then is a public one, and speaking the text is an act of persuasion intended to convince those listening and to win the case. It is crucial to each of you that you win this argument.

When you have tried it out, consider these questions:

- What does it feel like to place the scene within the context of a courtroom?

- Did you communicate your argument effectively, and if so, how did you do that?

- Did you use the space at all or did you simply stand still to deliver your lines?

- Did anything happen to your voice?

- Did you use gestures at all to emphasise your point?

Now explore the opposite and play the scene as if this is an exchange between two men who do not want anyone else to hear, but who desperately need to talk to each other. Keep in mind the relationship between the characters: this is a scene between a father and son. Emphasise the vulnerability of each within the relationship – perhaps Creon loves his son and wants his respect. Maybe Haemon loves his father and, as well as wanting to save his fiancée, is trying to prevent him from making a terrible mistake. The scene then becomes something personal and private, an intimate exchange between family members.

When you have spent time exploring the scene from this perspective, ask yourself these questions:

- How did this version compare to the previous one?

- Did you try and find some psychological motivation in order to play the scene, and were you able to do so?

- What happened to you physically during this version?

- Was the space used any differently?

- How was the delivery of the lines affected?

- How did you deal with the presence of the chorus?

Return to the text for a third time. Each of you needs to win the argument, which is actually an argument about how a city should be ruled, a very public issue. Remember that some of the lines are addressed to the chorus, who are present throughout. Do not forget, however, that you are father and son and that is the private bond between you – although it is also a relationship that is understood publicly. Explore the possibilities of combining the personal with the rhetorical. Feed off the conflict, look at what it does to you physically.

Is there a particular gesture or physical expression that would allow those watching to understand the attitude of each man in terms of their relationship to each other, and to the argument?

Be aware of the space between you, and how you close it down or open it up to make your point.

Try treating the words as weapons used to destroy the other's argument.

Don't lose sight of the intimate relationship running through the scene, the current keeping the rhetoric afloat.

Remember how high the stakes are right from the very beginning.

This exercise ought to have really challenged you to consider what style of acting best serves the text. We tend to view everything we read or see through our own cultural lens. As actors coming from within a contemporary Western tradition of actor training, you may well have wanted to go straight to the heart of the exchange between the two men by exploring their psychological motivations and trying to see how their characters develop as the scene progresses. You may, however, have been frustrated in your attempts to do so!

You need to remember that different texts ask different things of you. These texts from Ancient Greece, and others like them, are often formal in tone: there is no small talk or casual interplay between characters. As a result, every word you speak counts; you can't throw anything away. Short, single-line exchanges are interrupted by long, rhetorical speeches often reflecting on the political or philosophical. There are no props that you can fiddle with: objects are rare, and so assume huge significance and specificity within the story. You won't find comforting stage directions telling you to plump cushions on a sofa or clatter plates on a table. Often there is no build-up to the level of emotion that a character experiences.

They begin on a high, and then the intensity continues to grow. There are no physical habits or mannerisms that you can anchor your performance in. Where can you hide, then? Nowhere! This is acting laid bare, it is wonderfully exposing and you will need all your technique and strength to sustain it.

Do not fall into the trap of becoming very static and formal in your own explorations. Beware of adopting a grand voice in order to do justice to these grand thoughts! You will need to think about how to use the stage space and your body within it. No gestures can be casual – they are instead displays of power and persuasion – but that does not mean that you need to lose your inner life. Just because the characters are not *formed* with modern psychological impulses in mind, it does not mean that these stories do not focus on inner conflicts and human motivations. You can still explore the creative tension between a stylised presentation and the hugely psychologically fraught dilemmas faced by the characters.

There are many issues that arise for the actor when dealing with these sorts of plays, and you will need to adjust your thinking a bit. Do not separate the private from the public, instead get used to the fact that they always embrace each other in these texts. There is complete coherence in the scene you have just looked at between the intimacy experienced by family members and the theory of political power. These characters are used to the glare of public attention, they function within it, spilling their guts as they do so. Think of the many reality-television shows on our screens daily where seemingly private matters are unashamedly exposed to public scrutiny. These characters air their own disputes through an equally exposing lens!

Ultimately, the aesthetics of any production that you are in will influence your acting too. This genre can be viewed as entirely theatrical, but it is equally open to the possibilities of a realist approach. Whatever the choices are within a particular production, we know that these plays were written before the modern notions of psychology and motivation that are so present in our thinking today. The style of acting would also have had to be appropriate for the scale of the theatres the plays were staged in: these were vast spaces where small intimacies onstage would have been utterly lost to the spectators. You can see how important the use of mask and gesture might be in enabling the actors to communicate with their audience.

There is an interesting story involving a famous actor of the time. His name was Philus and he was playing the part of Electra, who has to weep copiously over an urn that contains the ashes of her dead brother. The character is experiencing unendurable grief at this point. Philus filled the urn with the ashes of his own dead son, and lamented over that onstage. People of the time apparently found his performance very moving. Here is an example of the way an actor made something personal way before there was any talk about psychological methods of engagement with a role!

As a result of this work you should:

- Continue to work responsively and boldly, using actions, objectives and given circumstances – where appropriate!

- Understand that different texts make different demands on you as an actor.

- Be able to explore the use of gesture in order to illuminate meaning within the text.

- Be able to take your relationship with the audience into account.

- Be able to approach text from a dramaturgical perspective.

- Be able to fuse a rich, dynamic inner life with a representation of the arguments particular to the scene.

- Be able to explore a text physically as well as intellectually.

- Feel more confident when approaching text that is particularly complex.

Shakespeare

Perhaps you remember back to your schooldays when you spent hours trapped in a stuffy room whilst a class-mate stumbled through a particular passage of Shakespeare, mangling its meaning in the process. Perhaps you have witnessed, as I have, performances of Shakespeare that have bored you rigid. Maybe you have never seen any Shakespeare performed because either it hasn't been available to you or because you haven't wanted to go, assuming that it will be old-fashioned and of no relevance to your life. Conversely, perhaps you are an avid fan of Shakespeare's work, you love the stories and the rich language, and have seen some great productions. Perhaps you have even had first-hand experience of performing it yourself. Either way, when you go to drama school, you will certainly come into contact with Shakespeare's work, working a great deal on complex poetic texts in voice and acting classes. It may well be that you explore Shakespeare's plays in your first year, but I am choosing to include this section as part of the focus on your second year of training.

The reason for this is that working on Shakespeare really exercises your muscles as an actor. It brings the elements of your training together as it requires you to connect emotionally, to explore character motivations, to consider given circumstances, to work responsively and boldly with those around you – but also to be aware of the way that the plays do not attempt simply to recreate everyday reality. In them, actors frequently speak directly to the audience; a small play may be staged within the larger one; contrasting scenes and plotlines are juxtaposed so that the audience has to pause and take stock of what is going on, rather than be allowed to get totally swept away by identifying emotionally with the world of the play. Of course, you also need to trust the language and learn to use it, so that it not only helps you to access the inner landscape of the character, but also so that you can communicate story, imagery and argument to your audience, enabling them to engage with the action onstage, not feel distanced from it.

Aims

- To consider the challenges faced by modern actors working on Shakespeare.

- To give you an idea of the sort of exercises you might be asked to engage with.

- To sharpen your responses to the text.

- To show you that the texts are full of possibilities for you to choose from.

- To encourage you to continue to work as you have done throughout your training so far by putting your concentration outside of yourself.

- To help you shake off any preconceptions of how Shakespeare *should* be played in order to get it 'right'.

- To get used to the idea of working things through slowly and noticing the cumulative effect that exercises have on you.

Problems for the Modern Actor

The challenges that face the modern actor are similar to those that face the modern audience. We are not used to listening to really long speeches. Obviously politicians still make lengthy addresses, but on the whole our use of, and reliance on, language has diminished. We are so used to the visual now – think about the advertising that we are constantly subject to, images and logos and brands. We are surrounded by posters, magazines, blocks of neon information, televisions, computers, hand-held screens. This plethora of visual stimulus means that we aren't required to listen as hard as we might have done in the past. In Shakespeare's day this was not the case. In the 1600s, printing was very expensive – and by no means everybody could read – so there would be no easy access to books. Paintings, apart from those in church, were generally only seen by the people who were invited to the wealthy households in which they were displayed. Because of this, communication relied on the spoken word in a way that it simply doesn't today.

The nature of the spoken word has also altered during the last four hundred years. Vocabulary is constantly changing, as words become obsolete and new ones come into use – ords like 'chillax' or 'bromance' can be heard regularly now, although they would have bewildered people if used in conversation only a few years ago. So how is the modern actor supposed to deal with words that were common four hundred years ago, but now offer different meanings... if they are used at all? Have a look at this little list to get a sense of what I mean:

Strossers – Trousers
Neb – Nose/Mouth
Quick – Alive

Tomboy – Prostitute
Round – Frank
Fond – Silly/stupid

At first glance the language might seem an obstacle to the modern actor. As a starting point try reading the plays out loud to yourself. Speak the language without stopping to wrestle with a word that you do not understand. Just think about who is speaking, and to whom? Ask yourself what they want, and why they want it at that particular point in the play? As a rule, pause briefly when there is a comma and for longer after a full stop, but otherwise simply keep going to get a sense of the meaning of the text. You will begin to find that the sounds and the rhythms become as important, if not more so, than what the words themselves actually mean. Shakespeare isn't around to ask, so now the language belongs to us, and we can only approach it from our own modern understanding. What it means is what it means to us. Don't be careful, don't be reverential. Kick that text around and you may find that some of the issues that you thought were blocking you will evaporate.

Sometimes actors think that they have a problem with a bit of text simply because they are working on Shakespeare, but sometimes Shakespeare is making that language difficult on purpose to make a point. Perhaps it is not the actor's struggle, but in actual fact it's the character's. When the language gets particularly difficult, there is usually a reason. Is the character in a bit of a spin emotionally? Is the character pompous and using language in an overly pretentious and complex way? Is the character blindly in love and not able to articulate clearly? Is the character so stupid his speech gets tangled up? Is he a peasant or a lord? Look at when the language seems naturalistic and when it doesn't. Listen to how other characters speak to your character and how that might influence your response.

In modern texts you need to think about what is going on in the gaps between the words as well as the words themselves, as subtext and meaning can happen in the silences as well as the sounds. When there is complexity of feeling in poetic text, it is expressed through the words themselves, and in the rhythms of the speech. The language is the only means of expressing what your character is going through, and once you understand how it is working then you may not find it so difficult to approach Shakespeare as a modern actor. Shakespeare himself was an actor – he would understand what you are going through!

Making It Your Own

For the purpose of clarifying the exercises, I will be using the Arden edition of *The Complete Works of Shakespeare* throughout this section.

Write out the text that you are working on in your own words. For example, the following passage from *A Midsummer Night's Dream* (Act One, Scene One):

> Call you me fair? That fair again unsay!
> Demetrius loves your fair: O happy fair!
> Your eyes are lode-stars, and your tongue's
>   sweet air
> More tuneable than lark to shepherd's ear,
> When wheat is green, when hawthorn buds
>   appear.
> Sickness is catching; O were favour so,

Yours would I catch, fair Hermia, ere I go:
My ear should catch your voice, my eye your
   eye,
My tongue should catch your tongue's sweet
   melody.
Were the world mine, Demetrius being bated,
The rest I'd give to be to you translated.
O, teach me how you look, and with what art
You sway the motion of Demetrius' heart.

Might become:

Are you calling me good-looking? Oh, don't
say that, because Demetrius likes your kind of
looks, not mine. You are so lucky to look the
way you do. Your eyes draw him in and your
voice sounds more beautiful than a lark
singing at the beginning of spring when
everything is green and the buds are just
coming out. You can catch illnesses, so I wish
that good looks and charm were infectious as
well. If you could catch that sort of thing,
before I did anything else, I would catch the
way you look, the way your voice sounds, the
way you sing. If I owned everything in the
whole world, except Demetrius, I would give it
all up if I could turn into you, because then he
would love me. Tell me what your appeal is.
How do you get him to fancy you? How do
you make him love you?

If you want to take this further, you could substitute all
the names of people and places in the text for those
that feature in your own world and life. So, for example, in the text that I have been using here, I would
substitute Demetrius for the name of a man that I really

like in real life, but who I know doesn't reciprocate my feelings!

Speak the text aloud, a thought or a phrase at a time, alternating between the character's words and your own.

You can see that, in my example, I have put the speech into my own words without changing its meaning, but very much using language that I can relate to and feel comfortable with. The process simply clarifies for you what is going on in the text and allows you to fully understand the intentions behind the speech. Take your time over this process. Often Shakespeare's lines are full of ambiguity, so when you substitute his words for your own, you should not attempt to make everything black and white; to nail the meaning down with utter surety when something less straightforward is going on. Convey a sense of what is happening as you understand it. The aim is to speak the text as if it was your own, and not something that you have found printed on a page and that is alien to you in some way.

Write Your Own

Shakespeare's verse is in *iambic pentameter*. 'Iambic' refers to the iamb, which is the name given to the basic beat. The stresses of an iamb go weak/**strong**, i.e. a weak syllable is followed by a strong one – tee-**tum**, tee-**tum**, tee-**tum**. If you think of words like he**llo**, good**bye**, rep**ort**, for**sake**, post**pone**, rec**eive**, cre**ate**, you can hear this stress pattern within the word.

'Pentameter' comes from the Greek words for 'five' and 'measure'. There are five iambs in every line, making a total of ten syllables in all.

Write your own sentences that follow the stress pattern of an iambic pentameter. Here are a few examples to give you an idea of what I mean:

/ _ / _ / _ / _ / _
I want to win the running race in June.

/ _ / _ / _ / _ / _
I hate it when it pours with rain all day.

/ _ / _ / _ / _ / _
I'd like a glass of whisky for my mum.

Finding the Stresses

As a starting point, look for the first stressed syllable within the line in order to understand the sense of what is being said. Locating this first stress enables you to get an insight into what is most important to your character at that point. Wherever possible, observe the iambic pentameter. Once you recognise the iambic pentameter you will also notice where the rhythms start to jump about, as the stresses cease to be regular. Sometimes a line contains an extra syllable, or one too few, so that you are unable to follow the regular stress patterns of the iambic pentameter. You may want to put two strong stresses side by side – **tum-tum**, or reverse the regular iambic stress pattern – **tum**-tee. The verse is there to steer you, but you must allow yourself the freedom to make the choices necessary to clarify meaning and to illuminate what is happening for your character emotionally.

Look at the following lines and read them over to yourself. Where does it feel right for you to put the stresses?

Write down each line and mark out the weak and strong stresses, as I have done in the examples I gave you earlier. Here are some speeches that you can use to get you started:

CHORUS.
 O for a muse of fire, that would ascend
 The brightest heaven of invention,
 A kingdom for a stage, princes to act,
 And monarchs to behold the swelling scene!
 Then should the warlike Harry, like himself,
 Assume the port of Mars, and at his heels,
 Leashed in like hounds, should famine, sword
  and fire
 Crouch for employment. But pardon, gentles all,
 The flat unraised spirits that hath dared
 On this unworthy scaffold to bring forth
 So great an object. Can this cockpit hold
 The vasty fields of France? Or may we cram
 Within this wooden O the very casques
 That did affright the air at Agincourt?

Prologue, Henry V

You would be hard pushed here not to stress the 'O' in 'O for a muse of fire', even though it falls at the beginning of the line, where you would expect an unstressed syllable to be. By kicking off the line with a stressed syllable in this way, the character is grabbing the audience's attention.

MACBETH.
    It will have blood, they say: blood will have
      blood:
    Stones have been known to move, and trees
      to speak;
    Augures, and understood relations have
    By maggot pies, and choughs, and rooks,
      brought forth
    The secret'st man of blood. – What is the night?

Act Three, Scene Four, Macbeth

In this speech you can see that the word 'blood' is repeated three times. In order to make sense of the point that Macbeth is making, you have to stress that word each time it occurs, regardless of what the regular iambic pentameter would dictate.

PHOEBE.
    Think not I love him, though I ask for him.
    'Tis but a peevish boy – yet he talks well –
    But what care I for words? Yet words do well
    When he that speaks them pleases those that
      hear.
    It is a pretty youth – not very pretty –
    But sure he's proud, and yet his pride
      becomes him.
    He'll make a proper man. The best thing in him
    Is his complexion; and faster than his tongue
    Did make offence, his eye did heal it up.

Act Three, Scene Five, As You Like It

Poor old Phoebe, although she starts using regular speech patterns, she soon departs from this form as she dwells more and more on the enchanting youth that she has just met.

You could carry on this exercise using other examples of text. The important thing is that the decisions you make about where to place the weak and strong stresses, you make knowingly. Think about the way a jazz musician has to be aware of the beat in order to go against it – you are in a similar position. It is essential, therefore, that you become adept at looking for the iambic pentameter.

Listening to the Language

Make sure you know what the particular section of text that you are working on means.

Sit in a circle with the rest of your group. Starting at the beginning of the speech, each person has a turn speaking the text out loud. They speak until there is a punctuation mark. At that point the next person in the circle takes over, and they speak the text up to the next punctuation mark, and so on. You may find that, when it comes to your turn, you only have one word before a punctuation mark crops up.

When it is your turn, do not be a robot and mechanically say your bit. You really need to listen to what has gone before so that you can pick up on the rhythm and flow and maintain it, before passing it on to the person sitting next to you.

Do the same exercise, only this time sing your section of text when it gets to your turn – but make sure that you are not all trying to sing the same tune. The text should be sung, but there should be no recognisable song emerging.

Do the exercise again but this time whisper the words.

When you do this exercise, you should pay attention to the rhythms of the thoughts. Some sections between the punctuation points will be longer than others, so when you get to a single word that sits between punctuation marks, consider what effect it has. How does it change the flow and what do you receive from that change? Did you get a sense of the meaning through noticing the rhythms? Did you notice whether the vowels in the words were long or short? How were you affected by this?

When you sang the words, what happened? Did people make different sounds as the meaning or emphasis in the text shifted? Whispering the text can feel very intense: was the energy of the speech affected by this?

Exploring without Words

You will need to work on texts that you have memorised and whose meaning you fully understand.

Sit on the floor blindfolded. Go through the speech you are working on, but instead of using words, deliver the speech by tapping or beating on the floor. You may also use breath and abstract sound, but avoid trying to be literal with the noises that you make.

If you are working on dialogue with someone else, sit opposite him or her. Both of you are blindfolded. Do the scene together, but again do not use words: instead use tapping, beating, breath and abstract sound to communicate what is going on for your character at that moment. Both of you should be influenced by the sounds you are hearing from your partner, as well as what is going on in relation to your own text.

You should not prepare for this exercise; simply commit to whatever noise you want to make, or rhythm you want to beat, in that moment. Those listening are unlikely to be able to understand every image or thought being explored, but they should get a sense of the emotional pulse within the character and within the scene. They should be able to hear shifts as the pulse quickens or recedes. They should be able to hear when the two characters are in tune and when their rhythms and tempos are at odds with each other. This work gives you direct access to how the text is working on an emotional level.

Lifting the Line

Simply kick a ball on the last word of every line of your text. That is not when the sentence comes to an end, necessarily, but the word at the end of each line as it is written on the page. For example, here is a bit of Hermione's speech from *The Winter's Tale*, when she is standing trial, accused by her husband of adultery. I have marked the point where you should kick in bold.

HERMIONE.
    Since what I am to say, must be but **that**
    Which contradicts my accusation, **and**
    The testimony on my part, no **other**,
    But what comes from myself, it shall scarce
      boot **me**
    To say 'not guilty'

            Act Three, Scene Two, *The Winter's Tale*

You need to be careful here not to anticipate your kick or wait too long to commit to it. You must not kick on the word before or after that last one in the line. The exercise reminds you not to settle at the end of the line but to keep driving the energy through, thereby enabling the speech to keep moving.

Vowels and Consonants

Use a speech for this exercise that everyone has learnt already.

Sit in a circle. The whole group now speaks the text together, but only vocalises vowels. Try and engage with the sense contained within each vowel so that the sounds do not come out of you empty and with no apparent meaning behind them.

For example, if you were looking at Lady Macbeth's speech in *Macbeth* (Act One, Scene Five):

LADY MACBETH.
    The raven himself is hoarse,
    That croaks the fatal entrance of Duncan
    Under my battlements. Come you Spirits
    That tend on mortal thoughts, unsex me here,
    And fill me, from the crown to the toe, top-full
    Of direst cruelty! make thick my blood,
    Stop up th'access and passage to remorse;
    That no compunctious visitings of Nature
    Shake my fell purpose, nor keep peace between
    Th'effect and it!

You would say:

> ER AY E I E I OAR
> A OA ER AY A E A O U A
> U ER EYE A E E. U OO II
> A E O OR A OR, U E EE EE,
> A I EE, O ER OW OO ER OE, O U
> O EYE E U E EE! AY I EYE U,
> O U A E A A AY OO E OR;
> A OE O U I OU I I I O AY URE
> AY EYE E UR O OR EE EE E EE
> E E A I!
>
> I have tried to communicate in this example the *sounds* that the vowels are making within the word.
>
> Now, together, speak the speech through in its entirety and notice what the vowels sound like having had that experience of isolating them.
>
> Repeat the exercise, but this time, collectively, sound out the consonants only.

You should find that you get a sense of Lady Macbeth's emotional journey when you sound out her vowels. Notice when the vowels are long and drawn out and when they fire from you in abrupt bursts. You should be able to see patterns emerging, which will give you an insight into the character's inner workings. It requires an effort to go through a speech like this, and through the physical action of making the sounds you may well find that you have an emotional response to them yourself. Long, drawn-out vowels feel very different to short jagged ones.

Similarly, with the consonants you can get an immediate sense of where the character is being forceful, the hard

Ks and glottal Ts and the explosive Ps. These contrast with the softer consonants, some of which are even devoiced, the breathy H and the hissing S. It really does allow you to gauge the emotional temperature of your character.

Drawing the Text

Use a speech that you are working on and understand the meaning of.

On a large sheet of paper, draw an image for every word of the text, even the little words like if and but. You do not have to draw a literal image, as that would be difficult with the joining words, you can use a symbol or a shape or a dash to express them.

Do this exercise slowly, allowing yourself time to really mull over each word before you commit it to paper.

This is not a free-association exercise where you quickly draw the pictures that come to you as you read the text. The purpose is to inhabit the words through the drawing, so take your time with it. When you have gone through the speech in this way you should be able to see how the words push against each other; they are not isolated noises. All the images you come up with should build towards a sense of the speech as a whole. Each word keeps the flow of sense moving until the final punctuation mark.

Landing the Thoughts

Stand facing a partner a few feet away. Each of you is working on a speech that you have memorised and understood for meaning. Label yourselves A and B.

Actor A: you will start the exercise by speaking the first line of your speech to actor B. Actor B: if you feel that that line has been fully communicated to you, say 'yes'. It will then be your turn to deliver your first line of text to actor A. If, however, you feel that you have not fully received the line, say 'no' and actor A will repeat it until you feel that it has been communicated to you. Only then will you say 'yes', and it will then be your turn. Go back and forth between you in this way until each of you has spoken the whole of your text.

You will find during this exercise that the way to communicate with your partner is not necessarily through volume. You can shout all you like, but it won't mean that the other actor will receive what you are saying. Instead, you need to focus on clarifying the thought so that your partner understands what you are saying. These are not generalised words that you are throwing about, but specific ideas, images and needs. If you get inside these and follow the thoughts through right to the end of the line, then you will pass them on to those listening to you. Don't be tempted to push or shout to make your point – just breathe and tell the story of the line.

When you do this exercise, do not try to direct your partner or give them tips on how to communicate better. Just say 'yes' or 'no' and nothing else.

Marking the Punctuation

Begin to read through your text out loud. When you are actually speaking, stand still. When you come across a punctuation mark walk, a little way. Every time you hit a punctuation mark, travel in a different direction to the way you previously walked.

This exercise can give you an insight into the mental state of your character at that point in the play. If you are feeling dizzy from all the changes of direction, then it is likely that your character is feeling the same way too!

Taking the Punctuation Away

Write the section of text that you are working on out on a sheet of paper. Do not include any of the punctuation marks, just copy out all the words.

Read the lines out loud to yourself, noticing where you need to take a breath.

As an example of what I mean, have a look at this extract from one of Macbeth's speeches. He is thinking about killing Duncan, the King, who is his guest for the night. I have written the lines out without any of the punctuation. Notice what happens: Macbeth starts quite logically, but then becomes swept up in the horror of what he is contemplating. I have marked out where I think that the breath might be taken. The capital 'B' in the fifth line is a clear indication of where to take a breath because it heralds a new thought within the line, but see if you agree with the rest of my breathing points.

MACBETH.
              He's here in double trust /
First as I am his kinsman and his subject /
Strong both against the deed / then as his
   host
Who should against his murtherer shut the
   door
Not bear the knife myself / Besides this
   Duncan
Hath borne his faculties so meek hath been
So clear in his great office that his virtues
Will plead like angels trumpet tongu'd against
The deep damnation of his taking off /
And pity like a naked new-born babe
Striding the blast or heaven's cherubins hors'd
Upon the sightless couriers of the air
Shall blow the horrid deed in every eye
That tears shall drown the wind /

                 Act One, Scene Seven, *Macbeth*

Because you are not relying on the punctuation to tell you where to breathe, you will be discovering this for yourself. The breath and the thought are inseparable. You take a breath when you have a thought. The amount of breath that you take will be dictated by the length of the thought and by what is at stake at that moment. The breath expresses the thought.

Release

You need to have memorised a speech to do this exercise.

One person stands in the middle of the room while the rest of the group form a circle around them. Make sure that the circle is close to the person in the middle and that there are no gaps in it.

The person in the centre speaks their text, while those on the outside push them around the circle. The person speaking, despite being jostled, should simply continue with the words and not stop to regain composure. They should pursue the sense of the speech despite being put off balance in this way.

As soon as you have gone through the text like this (more than once if the speech is a short one), the rest of the group moves away, and the person in the middle goes straight into the speech, this time without being jostled.

This is a good way of getting you to stop thinking too much. The action of being jostled in the circle can make you feel both energised and vulnerable, and this leads to a more immediate take on the speech. Of course, detail and precision might be lacking, but it is a very useful way of breaking you out of habitual patterns of speech and any tendency to overwork. As a group, you need to be careful not to push too hard. The actor in the centre, although destabilised, should feel safe, otherwise they will not be able to let go and to commit to the speech.

Distractions

Play the speech or the scene whilst carrying out a difficult task. Make sure that you focus on getting the task done as well as communicating the text. You have ten minutes to do this.

For example, you might count a pile of coins of all different denominations and add them all together in your head. You might balance a bamboo cane on your nose. You might build a five-storey house out of cards.

This is a useful exercise when you are getting too caught up in your head and need a distraction from the words, which may be becoming forced and overworked. When your mind is on something else, paradoxically you may find that the text starts to have more meaning.

Freedom to Express

Divide a speech up between the group so that everyone takes a phrase of it.

Now speak the text while walking around the room, everyone speaking their bit in the order it comes in the speech. Continue doing this for a while until everyone has a sense of the flow of the piece as a whole.

When you feel that this flow has been achieved, move in any way you like when you get to your bit of the text. You might feel like hopping or running, crawling or jumping, it really doesn't matter. Keep going through the speech in this way, letting your lines affect you freshly each time you come to them. The way you move will also affect how you speak, so you might find yourself begging, shouting or whispering – again it really doesn't matter.

When you have done this enough times to explore the possibilities fully, stop and stand still. Close your eyes and speak the whole of the passage through to yourself. See what has changed in you.

This exercise helps you to explore the text in a way that should liberate you from the need to be careful or poetic with the words. When you come to do the whole speech to yourself, it is interesting to see how much freer you are with it, not only the bit that was previously your own phrase, but also with the passage as a whole. You have been in a room full of people running and shouting, skipping and wailing; that may well be enough to release you from feeling reverential towards the text. When you come to the speech in its entirety, you might find a new energy within it, and all sorts of surprising things may be sparking in you.

Rapping

Go through a monologue that you are working on and know by heart. Rather than speaking it out loud, rap it instead.

You shouldn't plan how you might do this in advance, but instead just jump in and see what you discover about the rhythm and flow of the speech. You might find that you have an urge to repeat a line or a word – go for it. Allow yourself to be really playful. You may well be surprised to discover how easy it is to do the monologue in this way. This exercise helps you to 'make contact' with the rhythms in a speech, as it encourages you to be playful and bold with the language.

Responding

You need to have memorised the scene you are working on and to have understood its meaning.

If you are working on a scene with just one other person, then sit back to back with them.

Before you speak your line, speak the thought that may precede it. As an example, I have taken text from *Macbeth* (Act One, Scene Seven), and written the thought in italics above the actual line to show you what I mean.

LADY MACBETH.
   What the hell are you doing here on your own,
   drawing attention to yourself rather than
   playing the perfect host as we planned?

   He has almost supped. Why have you left the
      chamber?

Wait until the other person has finished speaking before answering them in your own words prior to responding in Shakespeare's.

For example:

MACBETH.
I just wanted time to think.

Hath he asked for me?

Play the entire scene in this way, answering each other in your own words before you proceed with your lines.

The lines that I have written in italics are examples only, you may have very different ideas about what the character is thinking before he or she speaks. That is fine: as long as you can support it through the text, there is no absolute right or wrong. This is simply a useful exercise to awaken your inner motors so that you are giving and receiving the lines in a way that is responsive, texturing your work with inner life. It is easy, sometimes, when we get caught up in the language and the imagery and the ideas, to start to work in a kind of bubble where we affect no one and are touched by no one. If you do not communicate with those around you, it is irrelevant how beautifully you speak the text: the audience will stop listening.

The Words Have Been Chosen

You will need to have memorised the speech and to understand its meaning. Using the actual text word for word, write the speech as if it was a letter to someone specific to the character. It is essential that every word you use in this letter is chosen with care, but imagine that you have not much time to complete it, even though the right words still have to be found.

This is a useful exercise to remind you that the words that make up the text are not chosen randomly, but serve a specific function in order to create an image, tell a story or communicate an idea. By writing the letter you get a chance to remember the significance of the words being used. Because you have a limited amount of time to achieve this task you have to be decisive and specific. The words should come to life as you use them to communicate with the person you are writing to.

Staying Alive

The group will need to have memorised the same speech.

Stand in a circle. Each person can say a word or a phrase from the speech in any order. No one knows who is going to speak next, but no one should speak at the same time. Practise this for a while until you feel comfortable with it.

Now do the same thing, but each word or phrase must follow on *in the order* that it comes in the speech. Bear in mind the punctuation and flow of the speech as you select the amount of text that you are going to say. No one knows who is going to speak next, but if two people or more speak at the same time then you must start at the beginning of the speech again. Try and speak the whole passage through in this way from beginning to end.

Clearly this exercise will keep you on your toes, as you will need to be focused and extremely aware of what is going on around you in order to get through the whole speech. The experience should channel your concentration as a group, but also make each individual within it very alive. This liveliness will, as a consequence, be injected into the speech. You should aim to allow the text to have a continuous flow and to avoid sounding robotic or hesitant as you share the lines. Commit fully to the words as you speak them.

Broadly speaking, these exercises have focused on form, imagery, release and connection. There are many other exercises that you will come across, and much of the work you did in the first year will also be useful. The most important thing is that you do not begin by thinking that Shakespeare's work is no longer relevant to you and that, as an actor, these texts require something beyond what you feel is accessible. Look at the play that you are working on as a whole and do not just focus on the role that you are playing. Look at the images that keep cropping up, at the recurring themes. See what the story is and find parallels with your own experience of the world and cultural view.

The imagery is expansive and you should not be frightened of expanding imaginatively with it. You don't need to be poetic with the text or to reduce it to something very careful and logical. Just as in everyday life we discover thoughts at the moment of speaking, here we discover the thoughts as we articulate the lines. The images used are not merely descriptive; they are active because they shape what is happening to the character and what is happening in the play as a whole. You need to engage fully with this and not distance yourself from it by being reverential with the text or feeling bound by it. Enjoy the language and trust that the verse is there to guide you and to ignite you. There is nothing fixed or rigid for you to feel trapped by. The language exposes the intentions and the thoughts and the emotional landscape of the character, as well as what is happening in that scene or the play as a whole.

These great plays are about human beings and all their complexities, contradictions and ambiguities. You really should take pleasure in the opportunities that they offer you as an actor.

By the end of this block of work, you should:

- Be able to inhabit Shakespeare's 'complex' language as you would your own.

- Be able to recognise verse form such as iambic pentameter.

- Be able to recognise that form and language affect your emotional landscape.

- Be able to play with the form with confidence.

- Be specific about the imagery and the argument.

- Be able to work responsively with heightened language.

- Be able to connect the breath to the thought.

Part Three
from Second
to Third Year:

Professional
Preparation

Professional Preparation

Having spent two years watching the final-year students perform, it is now your turn. This year marks a further transition in your training. Of course you will continue to learn and to explore, just as you will throughout your career, but now there is a new emphasis, now you will have your sights set on the years beyond drama school. You will need to be as prepared as possible.

During your third year you will perform in a series of public shows, or 'showcases'. This means that not only will your loved ones get a chance to see your work, but so will casting directors and agents. These productions have more than one function. Through them your training continues, but they also serve as a showcase for your work. The knowledge of this can cause you to become anxious, as you compare the parts you are cast in to other people's, worrying whether you are being shown in the best light or not. You may find that the atmosphere becomes rather more competitive than previously, and you must redouble your efforts to resist comparing yourself with anyone else. Focus on the play and your job within it instead.

Alongside the productions, there will be a series of sessions where you will work on acting for camera and radio. You will be given classes on audition techniques and sight-reading. You will be advised on getting great headshots. You will experience mock auditions. You will hear talks from people from the industry, including individuals who can tell you about things like paying your taxes when you leave. There will be competitions and festivals that you might be entered into. You will also be helped to prepare for a separate showing of speeches and duologues to a specifically invited audience of industry people.

In short, the aim of the year is to continue to develop you as actors, whilst preparing you for an industry that is renowned for its toughness. This is often the year when resentments can build up and anxieties become more pronounced. It is also the year in which you can begin to test the waters as an independent actor working with a range of directors and discovering more about your process. It is an exciting time!

Part Three has been divided into a series of questions and answers. Obviously, you are an individual and one answer doesn't necessarily fit all askers. However, these answers are the result of consulting various industry professionals, students and teachers, with the aim of making them as comprehensive as possible.

Aims

- To provide you with information about the industry.

- To tell you what you will need in order to approach agents and casting directors.

- To offer you advice for any meetings or auditions you might get called to. (Sometimes you won't be required to audition, but simply to meet a casting director, so that they can get an idea of who you are, and what sort of role you might be suitable for.)

- To address the issue of acting for television and radio as opposed to theatre.

- To encourage you to focus on what you are doing without comparing yourself to others.

- To prepare you for the showcase.

- To alert you to the fact that there may well be a written component to your final year.

Making Contact with the Outside World

As soon as you get cast in your first third-year production, you should write to agents inviting them to come and see the show. You will need to have had photographs taken so that you can include these, and your CV, with the invitation. No decent agent will represent you without first seeing you act, so these productions are good showcases, as well as providing you with a legitimate reason for contacting industry professionals

Headshots

What is the purpose behind these photographs?

On a very basic level, these photographs serve as a means of identifying you. They will go into Spotlight's database of actors and be referred to continually by casting directors and directors. Spotlight is an online site used by just about everyone linked to the profession. You will find their website address and details of their fees in the following chapter. You will also send photos to agents and directors yourself, although it is increasingly likely that agents and directors will look you up in Spotlight, which reduces the need to send photographs out, and so saves you some money. Photographs can also be printed on the top corner of your CV, so again the need for you to send out expensive prints is diminished. Often the photograph is the first view of you that a casting director gets, so as well as identifying you it needs to *sell* you too. You need to think of yourself in business terms: your photo is your calling card, and on it decisions may well be made as to whether to call you in for a casting or not.

How do I know which photographer to choose?

It is very important that you choose a photographer with experience in taking actor headshots. You may have a friend or relative who takes great pictures, but it is worth paying the money for a professional because they really know the market that they are taking the photograph for.

Look at as many photographs of actors as you can. You can do this by flicking through the Spotlight volumes of actor's photos or by trawling the internet. See which pictures you like and who took them. A photographer should not only be concerned with lighting and composition, but they should also be able to relax you so that the experience of having your photograph taken is enjoyable – these are the photographers that get the best shots. Your drama school can give you advice and will recommend photographers regularly used by previous students.

What size should my photograph be?

10" x 8".

Should it be colour or black and white?

It is more usual to have your photograph taken in black and white with a matt or gloss finish, although I think that the matt finish looks better.

What should I wear?

Bring at least three tops to your photo shoot. Avoid bold patterns and fussy collars as these can distract from the most important aspect of the picture, which is your face. Opt for a simple neckline. Black, white and grey are good colours to choose.

What if I have a spot?

Blemishes like spots and bruises are temporary so the photographer will retouch them. Moles and scars and other permanent marks should be left alone.

Should my picture be taken in a studio, indoors in natural light, or outside in natural light?

Everyone is different. Your skin tone and colouring react differently in different lights. Sometimes pale skin is better in a studio, whereas darker skin can soak up more light and so may look great outside, but this varies. Look at pictures of actors with similar colouring to you. Discuss the options with your photographer who can advise you. It may be the case that your photographer will take shots in a studio and also in natural light so that you can choose from either once you have seen the results. You can ask them to do this.

Should I try and look a particular way in the picture?

An experienced photographer will be able to capture your individuality and personality. A good picture should look like you on a good day. Don't try and be anything that you are not.

How much will it cost?

Naturally this will vary from photographer to photographer. You should expect to pay around £250, although there are photographers who charge in excess of £300, and some who offer sessions for as little as £100. Don't feel tempted to choose a photographer who is particularly cheap on the basis of price alone. You are making an investment here. However, paying exorbitant prices, way over the average rate, will not necessarily ensure you a significantly superior picture. Your college may have a deal going with a particular photographer who will work at a special discounted rate if it is a group booking.

Curriculum Vitae

What is it and what is it for?

A curriculum vitae, or CV for short, is a way of providing casting directors, directors and agents with information about you. It lists your physical attributes, experience and special skills as well as your contact details. An actor's CV is unusual in that it does not need to contain information that is not related specifically to the profession. So, for instance, listing all your academic achievements up until this point is of little interest to people who might be thinking of auditioning you.

How long should it be and what should it look like?

An actor's CV should be no longer than a single side of A4 paper. You should attach it to your headshot so it should be no bigger than that. Do not use fancy paper or swirly fonts to draw attention to it. Agents and casting directors receive literally hundreds of CVs every single week; anything that is not clear and concise will serve as an irritation to them rather than an attention-grabber.

Use black ink printed on decent paper: you want it to look as professional as you can.

What information should I include?

Print your name in big bold letters across the top and provide your reader with more than one means of contacting you; email as well as mobile and landline. If you already have an agent at this stage, then print their details rather than your own. You can also include a small headshot on your CV at the top of the page.

You will need to state your height, build, hair and eye colour and 'playing-age range' (i.e. the oldest and youngest ages you can convincingly act), so that whoever is reading your CV will get a physical impression of you to support the photograph.

State your native accent and list any other accents that you are able to do.

State where you are training and list your acting experience up to this point at college, naming the role, the play and the director.

In a separate section you can list other acting experience, such as productions you may have been involved in prior to drama school. Be judicious, though, and only list what is interesting or impressive: roles you played when you were in Year Seven at school do not count! Keep film and television credits, if any, separate from your theatre ones. Put any professional credits ahead of the amateur ones. Your credits should take up most of the page, but you don't want to cramp them up too much to fit them in. Discard the least interesting or impressive and keep the rest in neat columns.

Under the heading 'Skills', list any associated talents that you have. For example, horse riding, clean driving licence, grade 5 piano, jazz intermediate, fluent French, strong soprano singing voice, fight certificate, etc.

Finally, you can have a heading titled 'Interests': you may be keen on stand-up comedy, or have written a film script, or run theatre workshops for kids, or play in a band. These interests may or may not be directly related to the part you want to audition for, but they offer a useful insight into your personality.

Here is an example to give you an idea of how your CV might look:

Photo	**Rosa Jones** Mobile: 07... Landline: 0208... Email: rjones@...

HEIGHT: 5ft 10ins

BUILD: Medium

EYE COLOURING: Green

HAIR COLOURING: Black

PLAYING AGE: 22–26

ACCENTS: Birmingham (native); RP

TRAINED AT: Special School for Talented Actors

EXPERIENCE AT COLLEGE:

Role	Play	Director
Lady Macbeth	*Macbeth*	Isobel Thaler
Rachel	*Port*	Oscar Reiss
Olga	*The Three Sisters*	Jack Stringer

SKILLS: Piano Grade 5. Fluent French. Clean driving licence. Singing range: soprano.

INTERESTS: Athletics, stand-up comedy, scuba-diving.

I haven't done anything really, apart from the college productions, although I was an extra for a film once and did some riding when I was a child. Shall I embellish it all a bit to fill in the gaps?

NO!!! Do not lie on your CV. Agents and casting directors will know that you are just leaving college and so will be less experienced; they will not be expecting a great list of credits. Do not bump up a non-speaking role, and it's better not to include any extra or walk-on experience on your CV. If you say you have been an extra then you may begin to be viewed as one. You will find in the profession that people are very quick to categorise you with the result that it can be difficult to climb out of the pigeon-hole that you have been put in. If you try and embellish the extra work and make it sound like it was a featured role then you will be found out. It is a small world out there, and you are likely to run into someone connected to the film you have mentioned. It would be very embarrassing to be discovered in a lie.

Similarly, unless you really can do something well, do not list it as a skill. People will get extremely annoyed if they think that you can gallop bareback on a horse, only to discover that you managed a trot on a tired old Shetland pony when you were eleven. This goes for everything on your CV, whether you are listing accents, singing range, stage combat or playing age.

Should I include a cover letter with my CV and photograph?

Yes, a short letter that fleshes out some of the information included on your CV should be sent too. Keep it pithy but also relevant, either to the agent you are seeking representation from, or the part you want to audition for if you are writing to a casting director. Make sure you have done your research and include anything that you think they will find especially interesting or useful. The letter should give an insight into who you are, but must not become an essay on your life or be at all pleading or apologetic. Do not write things like 'It is my dream to become a professional actor,' or 'It is my dream to share the same agent as Ben Whishaw.' Everyone has dreams but not everyone has the talent and discipline to be an actor. Focus instead on what is real and purposeful. So, for example, invite the agent to see you in a production, or mention someone on their books that you respect as an actor, and say why. If you are writing to be considered for a part, talk about having seen a particular production by the company you wish to audition for.

Agents and theatre companies receive hundreds of these letters a week; they simply haven't the time to read pages and pages of irrelevant information. You want them to come and see your work and you want to present yourself in a positive light so they will call you in. It is as simple as that. Keep all covering letters short and to the point.

Emails are used more and more now as a means of communication in the industry. Again, keep these concise and specific.

Getting an Agent

You should aim to be signed up with an agent before you leave drama school, although it is certainly not the end of the world if you don't. It is crucial that you feel as prepared and confident as possible in understanding the role your agent will play in your career, and what to expect from them. It may not feel like it when you are first starting out as an actor, full of gratitude that an agent has taken you on in the first place, but this is an equal partnership, in which you are paying for your agent's services. The relationship requires mutual respect. Before you agree to be represented by anyone, make sure you understand the nature of his or her business.

Are there major differences between the agencies?

Yes, and not just between the individual agents themselves, some of whom you might feel more comfortable with than others. There are differences between the agencies themselves, in terms of size, status and function. It might be an advantage to go with a large, prestigious agency, but if you are fresh from drama school you may find yourself overlooked as the agent focuses on well-known clients instead. A smaller agent may be able to offer you more personal attention, but check that their client list is proportionate to the number of people they have working within the agency. Some have too few staff to adequately serve the great quantity of actors on their books. There are also specialist agencies, which represent specific kinds of acting work:

Cooperatives usually have about twenty actors within a cooperative agency. They take it in turns to run the agency when they are not acting, with one full-time manager supervising.

Large agencies represent models, presenters, etc. Be careful of such agents unless you want to go into the areas of work that they specialise in. They are not suitable for actors who do not want to model or present.

Casting agents provide film and television with extras and walk-on, non-speaking parts which do not need to be auditioned for. Obviously this is not the sort of agency that you require.

Voice-over agents concentrate on getting you voice-over work for film, television and radio. Not all agencies have a voice-over department so it may be necessary to employ a separate agent to secure you work in this area.

If an agent asks to see me, does that mean that they want to represent me?

It is a very positive sign if an agent invites you for a meeting, as it means that you have got something that they are interested in. However, representation is not guaranteed. When they meet you they might realise that you are similar to someone they already have on their books. (An agent won't want to represent too many people from the same casting pool: if they already have an amazing Amazonian blonde actor on their books, they may not feel that they can serve another, since both actors would always be going up for the same part.) They might be interested in you but not have space for you at the moment. Often they will want to see some more of your work. If they have called you in after your initial third-year production, they might want to see more shows before making a decision about you. You should feel reassured that an agent is taking the trouble to be certain before offering you representation; it means that when they do make an offer, they are doing so because they really want you on their books.

You might also want to wait and meet other agents before making your mind up about representation. It is really important that you sign with an agent, not with an agency. It may be that whoever you speak to from a big, impressive agency does not make you feel as confident as someone from a smaller agency does. Trust your instincts: many smaller agencies can get your career off to just as good a start as a big agency can. It is the particular agent within the organisation who you will be in contact with, so it is essential that you feel a rapport with that person.

What should I wear for a meeting with an agent?

You should wear something comfortable that also looks good on you. You don't have to be as formal as you might in a regular job interview, but you always want to show yourself off to best advantage. Don't pile on the make-up or wear vertiginous heels. Don't wear the suit that your mum bought you for your sister's wedding, but now feels very tight across the shoulders. Don't have hair falling into your eyes. Don't look shabby. Choose something that suits you and makes you feel relaxed and good about yourself.

How many people from drama school do agents take each year?

This will vary from agency to agency according to who they have on their books at that point. One agent that I spoke to said that, though she did go to see student show-cases, on the whole she preferred to take actors a couple of years after they had graduated from drama school, because by then they will have discovered how tough it is and will have a stronger understanding of what they are about. However, the majority of agents I spoke to said that they took between one and three people a year.

Is there any advice that I should bear in mind when I meet an agent?

Prepare well – know about the agency you are going to see. Be positive about yourself and your work, but do not be dishonest about what you have done. Some of the traits that agents have mentioned to me that they dislike in an actor they are meeting for the first time are: arrogance, bitterness, lack of self-awareness, lack of preparation, being over-apologetic. One agent I spoke to said that she needed to feel that she could go on a journey with a prospective client, so you should make sure that you come across as a great travelling companion! Recently she ran a couple of audition days at a drama school and said that the experience really brought home to her how important personality is. The majority of the students that she saw did fantastic audition speeches, so it came down to the five minutes of chat with each student to discover who stood out. She wanted to see who would be the person that a director would most want to be in a rehearsal room or on a film set with.

When you are nervous, you can sometimes come across in ways that are not actually representative of who you are and what you are really like. You should give this some thought – think about how you would like to come across and work towards that. A great deal of how you are received by other people rests not on what you say but on your body language. Do you smile when you first meet someone as if you are pleased to see them? When you sit down, do you perch on the edge of your seat nervously, or do you lean right back in the chair, inviting someone to come to you rather than making the effort to engage with them? When you feel uncomfortable, do you cross your arms or hug yourself? Do you maintain good eye contact with the person you are talking to, or do you either keep glancing away or staring them down? Is your body angled towards the person you are meeting, indicating an interest in what they are saying, or is it angled away as if you would rather keep them at a distance? You can consciously work on some aspects of your body language so that you come across as open, confident and attentive as possible, even when this is not how you are feeling.

What you say is also important. Speak clearly and not too fast, and if you are prone to apologising for yourself, banish the word 'sorry' from your vocabulary. Think of some questions to ask so that you won't feel at a loss for what to say. They are probably going to ask you something about your experiences at college, your interests, or what you see your strengths as an actor to be. Anticipate some of the questions so that you are ready for them. Keep relaxed; remember that *they* have asked *you* to come in, so you are a welcome guest. You also need to gauge how you feel about the agent: it is a two-way process, in which each of you is assessing the other, so take some of the pressure off yourself.

Resist urges you might have to be very negative about people who you have worked with. Recently I watched as an important director stopped to chat to a student that he thought had been good in a show; he was thinking of asking her to audition for his next project. He asked her how she had found the production she had just been in. Immediately she was negative, she complained about the script, the direction, her casting. Before my eyes, the director's initial interest in her began to dwindle. Of course, you don't have to be positive and cheerful about everything, but there is a way of voicing issues that is interesting and implies that you are engaged in a process. When you meet an agent you don't have to say that everything is wonderful, but do not depress them with complaints – and certainly don't start blaming anyone for something that hasn't gone right. If you are blaming your teachers for your casting or the other actors for not quite supporting you, then the agent will assume that you will start blaming them if your career doesn't go exactly to plan.

If they say 'keep in touch', should I, or do they say that to everyone?

Agents are far too busy to want people they have no interest in to contact them, so, yes, if they ask, you should keep in touch. This doesn't mean frantic phone calls to see whether they are ready for you yet. Keep them informed of the productions that you are in, and invite them to come and watch your work.

Will the agent ask me to do a speech?

It is very unlikely that an agent will ask you to do a speech for them. They are more interested in talking to you and getting a sense of your personality and how you come across. However, never say never! Have one prepared just on the off-chance.

Should I ask questions?

Yes, you should find out as much as you can about any potential representation.

If you don't already know, you could ask questions about how long they have been going as an agency; how many clients they have on their books; what their attitude to profit-share or low-paid theatre work is; what their rates of commission are. You shouldn't interrogate the agent, but you do need to get a good sense of who they are and how they go about their work so that you can be confident in your choices and understand what you can expect from them. An agent could reasonably assume that you have consulted their website before coming to see them; don't ask unnecessary questions that have already been addressed on it.

Will an agency ask for money up front?

A cooperative agency may ask for joining fees, but no other legitimate agency should. If you are asked for money by an agency other than a cooperative, do not pay it. No registration or up-front fees are asked for by bona fide agencies.

What's the difference between an agent and a personal manager?

This can get a little confusing, as often agents include the word 'management' in their title. Basically, an agent uses their contacts to get you auditions and negotiates your pay once you have got a job. A personal manager checks out schedules and arranges press interviews, etc. The line between them does get blurred, but I don't think you need to be overly concerned with the distinction at this point.

How can I be sure that I have found the right agent?

You should look closely at their website and ask friends and tutors. Also look to see what other actors the agency has on its books and where those actors are working. If you look at the Spotlight website you will find a section on career advice, which includes a list of independent advisors who, for a small fee, will be able to talk your options through with you. What it boils down to, however, is how *you* feel about the agent and the agency. Were you comfortable talking to them? Were you impressed? Did they seem busy and efficient? Did you like them?

Can I have representation from more than one agent?

No. Within a particular agency there may be different departments for theatre, film and television, but the agency that you choose will be your sole representatives. Can you imagine how much chaos and squabbling there would be if this wasn't the case? It is okay to have a separate voice-over agent, however, as these are often distinct agencies focusing only on voice-over work.

What is different about a cooperative agency?

There are over fifty cooperative agencies in the United Kingdom, with about twenty members in each. Some of them are excellent. Although they may not be viewed as having as much status as more conventional agencies, if they do offer you representation do not dismiss the opportunity. These agencies are non-profit-making: the actors within the agency take turns in running the office and any commissions that come in are used to cover the administrative costs. The commission you are charged when you are in work is likely to be lower than conventional agencies take, but you may be asked to pay a joining fee or monthly or annual payments in order to cover costs. If you do join, make sure that you know about all the members of the coop, and what parts they are likely to be cast in, so that you can see how you would fit in with the group. Communication needs to be excellent between members, as casting directors calling up will not want to find themselves repeating what they said to a different member on shift the day before. You will need to be able to manage the office skills required, and you have to be available to take your turn in the office and attend any meetings when you are not in work.

If an agency offers me representation, will I need to sign a contract?

This varies but if there is a contract read it through carefully. Check what commission rates are charged and also look out for a clause about the period of notice that you are required to give should you want to leave the agency. This period of notice is usually three months, but occasionally it can be longer: even as much as a year. Although at this point of your training it may not seem so important, a year is a long time to be stuck with an agent you are not happy with.

Are all agents based in London?

No, not at all, there are agents based throughout the United Kingdom, although a critical number are based in London. Have a look in *Contacts*, which is the book that Spotlight publishes, and that you can order via their website. Here you will find a full listing of all the agents, as well as other valuable information.

What is a casting director?

These are important people as they liaise between directors and agents, suggesting actors for particular roles for film and television and larger theatre companies.

Although they do not have the final decision on who is cast (that remains the domain of the director and the rest of the creative team), they are influential. If a casting director thinks you are good and appropriate for a role, then they will bring you in to meet the people who might give you the job. When you are watching anything on stage or screen, look to see who the casting director is. Familiarise yourself with names, where they work and who they cast for. Knowledge of the industry helps you prepare for it.

Acting for Camera

Will I be able to use my training so far and apply it to acting in front of a camera? So much of what I have done seems to have been geared for theatre.

It may well be that you begin working in front of a camera during your second year of training, but certainly during your final year you will get the opportunity to gain further experience. Of course, your previous training is still applicable, but it is easy to forget about your process when confronted by a camera and microphones and people saying 'Action!' just as you imagined they would! Specialist tutors and film and television directors will help you with all the new technical things that you will have to be aware of, but as well as this you should draw on your previous training and the process that you are discovering for yourself as a result of it. For example, look at what the script is saying, and how your character is functioning within it. What role do you play in making the story happen?

Go through all the given circumstances that you can glean from the text, for example:

- Is it hot or cold?

- What time of day is it?

- Where are you?

- Where have you just been?

- What is your objective?

- What is in your way?

- What are you doing to get what you want, and to what extent?

- What is your tempo and rhythm, inner and outer?

- What do other characters say about you and what do you say both about yourself and them?

- What characteristics do you possess and where do these contradict themselves?

You will need to use your imagination; you will need to listen and respond in the moment and impulsively. Ensure you play the action, not the emotion.

This is all familiar territory, and, although it may seem obvious now, it is amazing what goes out of the window when you are confronted by the unblinking eye of the camera and the quiet of the studio.

I have seen actors become oddly muted in front of a camera, as if this is a more truthful way of being. But it isn't necessarily. You must feel free to react without fearing that you are being too large. It is still all about the interaction between the actors, while the camera observes everything that is going on with just one eye as opposed to the many eyes that watch you in the theatre. You don't need to hold a moment to allow for the audience's laughter. You don't need to draw the audience in vocally or by picking out individuals to address. But that doesn't mean you have to consciously work to make everything smaller. The camera picks up all the thoughts that you are having, so be specific with your wants and really allow yourself to be driven by them. The stakes are often extremely high in film and television, so there is no need to reduce the size of your thoughts or of your desires. You simply do not need to communicate these to a wider audience, and you can use your normal register when talking to other people, as there is no call for projection. On the other hand, do not be tempted to devoice because things are more intimate. When you devoice, you make a sound that would usually be voiced, but you do it without vibrating your vocal chords. As a result your speech becomes softer and lighter, but it is an unnatural way of speaking and it shuts down your ability to really connect to what you are saying. Use your normal voice at the volume that the scene requires.

You will learn about continuity: handling props in the same way in each take and remembering where you moved, so you don't do something radically different from what you did in a previous shot. This means that, when edited together, the takes will join up seamlessly. Your teacher will talk to you about not rattling change in your pocket or slamming a car door at the same time as you speak so that the words are obscured. They will suggest that you don't blink too much and that you allow your whole face to be seen, unless your character is hiding for some reason. They will help you to control fussy unnecessary gestures so that your hands do not keep coming in and out of the frame. They will show you how to find your mark, a point on the floor that you must reach in order to be in shot. There are many technical things that you will learn, and the more you practise these, the easier it will become, so that ultimately the craft of the technique becomes one with the creativity of the acting. You might even practise with a video camera at home, so that you can watch yourself and note how the camera picks up on all your shifts of thought and desire, observing your inner life.

Students tell me that they find the lack of rehearsal time surprising when they start working on scenes for their television classes. As a result, they have to work independently and arrive at decisions quite quickly. Trust that you have the ability and tools to work in this way.

Radio

I hardly ever listen to plays on the radio; I am worried that I haven't got the right voice for it.

You should by now be listening and watching all sorts of things that perhaps you haven't previously been drawn to. Spend time listening to the radio, and you will hear a range of accents and sounds coming from it. You will be taught acting for radio by a specialist teacher, but notice the classes are in *acting* for radio – this isn't just a voice thing! You may well be surprised at how physical the classes are. You will be expected to sit like your character, lie like your character, even run like your character! This will all have to take place within a tight and specifically allocated space that is within the appropriate range of the microphone. You will learn new vocabulary and, importantly, you will have a chance to negotiate microphone technique, which can take a while to master. How you angle your head will change the quality of your voice, so you will have to gain an understanding of how you hold yourself in relation to the microphone.

Although finding this new medium fairly daunting to begin with, students have reported that they also found the sessions fun as they offered them a chance to play people that weren't like them at all in terms of age and demographics. No one can see what you look like, so you can be any one at all!

You will be expected to do *cold* readings, which means reading from a script that you have not previously looked at. Your teacher will help you to find strategies in coping with this, and I have included some advice for effective sight-reading in the following section of this book. There are things you can actively do to help you with sight-reading, so there is no need to panic even if you are dyslexic and feel that you do not function well in these circumstances.

Practise reading out loud at home as much as you can and from a variety of texts, such as newspaper articles, passages from novels, information from the side of your breakfast-cereal box. Read children's stories aloud: these will often encourage you to make instant decisions about characters and allow you to play with voices and accents.

As well as gaining microphone technique and confidence in your sight-reading, by the end of this work you should have a greater understanding of your own voice and the qualities that are peculiar to it, allowing you to see what sort of voice-over work you might be suitable for.

The Showcase

What is it?

Different drama schools may have different names for this event, but it is basically a further opportunity in your final year of training to be seen by an invited audience of industry professionals, for whom you will perform monologues, duologues and songs. Agents and casting directors will be invited to all your third-year productions, but this event is aimed at an audience of industry professionals alone. It usually takes place over the course of a lunch hour, allowing busy people the time to leave the office to come and see you. Your college will provide them with sheets of paper or pamphlets with photographs and names on, and the titles of the plays from which the speeches and scenes come. Be prepared for a lot of shuffling of papers and turning of pages during the performance. The sole reason for this event is for agents and casting directors to see who you are and whether they might be interested in you. If the performance is entertaining and has artistic merit, then that is a bonus for those watching, but they have not come to have a lovely time: this is very much the business end of things and you need to be prepared for that.

I am really worried about getting it wrong and messing up this opportunity. How do I know which pieces will sell me the most effectively?

This is very hard: every year some students get upset and anxious when trying to choose what they are going to do in front of this rather daunting audience. Often students think that this is their one chance to shine, and that if they don't bag an agent on this occasion, then they will never get another opportunity. This is simply untrue. Some actors start slowly and do not get a break till after they have left drama school. Some get many offers of representation, and everything looks exciting, but then nothing becomes of them in their career. If you can put it into perspective a little then you will take some of the pressure off yourself, and the choice of which pieces to pick will become a little less agonising.

Some drama schools allow you to do one piece only, either a speech or a duologue. If you are a very impressive singer then you may be allowed to sing too. Other drama schools allow you to do more than one piece, but either way your stage time will be very limited. Agents and casting directors will become impatient if they have to sit watching students for too long: they simply haven't the time. In this context, agents do not need an awful lot of time to know whether they are interested or not. So much of this goes on what you look like and who they already have on their books. Of course, you have to be good too, but don't get stressed out because you don't feel that you have been allowed enough time to be properly seen. Two or three minutes can be quite long enough in this context, although it may not feel that way when you are up there performing.

Your tutors will advise you about choosing pieces that sell you. Always choose something well written; it is difficult for even the best actors in the world to make a piece of bad writing sparkle. Try to pick something with a good dynamic that shows your ability to shift your pace, tone and focus. Don't forget that the point of all this is to sell yourself. Think how you might be cast professionally, and don't shy away from choosing something that reflects this. There is no point picking a piece that forces you to go against type. You don't get points for managing to play a role that you would never be offered. Look at actors similar to you and see what sort of roles they get cast in. Think about the sort of texts you have enjoyed working on. If you choose a scene or speech that you love, then you will find this whole experience easier. If you enjoy what you are doing, the audience are so much more likely to enjoy it too. You will not find one speech or scene that will show every aspect of who you are or what you are capable of, even two contrasting pieces will not provide you with the opportunity to do that. You are capable of much more than can be seen in a showcase, and everyone knows that – so keep calm, be practical, commit to the choices and try to relish your time onstage; that is really all you can do because the rest is beyond your control. Students often say that the showcase experience feels very much like a cattle market. It is certainly unlike any other element of your training, which has been con-cerned with exploration and self-discovery. Part of being an actor, though, is about taking your moment and delivering what has been asked of you. Here you have the opportunity to do just that.

Are there any speeches or scenes that put agents off?

You will not please everyone with your choices. However, the agents that I asked said that they found anything too 'heavy' within the context of the showcase unappealing. Sitting in the dark listening to great swathes of text about child abuse or grief can be quite hard after a while. That is not to say that you should only choose light, frothy material: simply do not get bogged down with heavy, emotional stuff that alienates an audience that is having to watch speech after scene after speech. If you do choose something that has a difficult content, then think carefully about delivering it so that it reaches and stimulates your audience without causing them to want to rush to the bar for a swift gin! The agents I talked to also disliked anything that involved a great deal of shouting, and they advised actors to avoid doing classical pieces unless they are absolutely brilliant. The audience wants to feel pleased that you have come on to the stage; they want to feel that they are in a safe pair of hands.

Some plays are very overused, which means that you have to do extraordinarily well with them to stand out. For example:

- *DNA* by Dennis Kelly

- *Punk Rock* by Simon Stephens

- *Breathing Corpses* by Laura Wade

- *4.48 Psychosis* by Sarah Kane

Don't forget that the agents go to lots of showcases, which means they hear some speeches time and time again. Students often think that they are being original by doing a piece from a play that has just opened at the Royal Court or the Bush, but inevitably someone from every drama school thinks the same thing. Look at what was going on at those venues five to ten years ago as well as in the last twelve months, so that you are not saturating your audience with pieces they have heard many times before. Your drama school will offer lots of advice, and they will shape a programme out of the excerpts in order to present everyone in the best light.

How will I know if an agent is interested in me?

It is customary for your college to provide food and drink for the agents after the showcase. This gathering offers you the chance to introduce yourself and for the agents to see what you're like in a different context. Students talk about feeling awkward in this situation, unsure of whether to go up to people. There will be staff from the college there to help you out and to make introductions for you, but if no one talks to you over the wine and canapés, it doesn't mean that you will not get representation or castings as a result of the showcase. Try to mingle as much as you can, make the most of having so many people from the industry to talk to and ask questions of. Present yourself in a relaxed and positive light, but if no one is actively seeking you out, don't lose heart. The reason for this is because agents, casting directors and directors are busy people and many of them simply can't hang around. The showcase also gives agents an opportunity to talk amongst themselves, which they may well find preferable to being interrogated by a student. If an agent or casting director wants to call you in, they will contact your college and you will be notified; you can then contact them to arrange a meeting.

It's also worth bearing in mind that casting directors may not be casting anything at that time that you would be suitable for. If they think you are interesting they will file your details and contact you when something appropriate comes up. I have heard actors say that they got a call from a casting director a year after they had done their showcase!

When you are thinking about what to wear for a gathering like this, don't show off too much flesh and don't slather on the make-up. Present yourself in the best light, show yourself off but be tasteful in how you do this –

many of the same rules apply as they did for the audition for drama school in the first place.

I haven't heard from any agents, should I call them myself?

Agents vary. Some don't mind taking calls from students at all and some do. A lot of them said that they preferred emails, but to send more than two would be excessive. Generally, if an agent wanted to represent you, they would have already got in touch, and so contacting them may not achieve much. However, many agents are open to giving advice, so if you contact them and ask if you could get some feedback on how you came across in the showcase, a lot of agents will help with this. It depends how busy they are. Their advice might prove really useful, plus if you do have a chance to talk to an agent then at least you have touched base with them – and if you are then in a show you can use this as a point of reference and invite them to come and watch your work. If they liked you when they met you and you are great in the show, then perhaps the nature of your relationship will change.

The marketing department at your college will have a list of all the agents who were present at the showcase so you will know who to get in touch with.

Competitions

Are there competitions and events that I might get involved with in the third year?

Yes there are, but before I go on to mention some of them it is important that you are prepared for the fact that your college might not choose you to enter into any of them.

Your teachers decide who is appropriate for each competition. For some, such as the Carleton Hobbs Radio Competition, decisions are relatively straightforward: actors are chosen because they have a particular aptitude for the medium being tested. Other competitions and events are less clear-cut. Do not let yourself be affected by the fact that some people are selected for these opportunities and some are not. Sometimes decisions are made for reasons that you are not privy too. Perhaps one actor hasn't had any luck with agents yet, perhaps they are more commercial than another, perhaps they are more comfortable with verse-speaking, etc. If this book has one piece of advice that keeps cropping up, it is not to compare yourself to others. A very prestigious agent that I spoke to said that actors should try to feel genuine happiness for someone else's success. He pointed out that jealousy rarely helps the person feeling it. Obviously this can be hard, as we are not always in control of how we feel, but there is no point thinking too much about something that you can do nothing about. If you don't get picked, focus on whatever you are working on and the moment will pass.

The Carleton Hobbs Radio Competition

This competition has taken place every year since 1953. Carleton Hobbs was a distinguished radio actor.

The drama schools choose four final-year students to enter this competition, usually two men and two women. Each team of four performs two rehearsed duologues with a combined time of no more than six minutes. They get feedback on these from the panel before doing them one more time. The judges are looking to see how well they interact with each other.

Each actor then does two contrasting monologues. Both of these speeches put together should last no more than four minutes. Judges will be listening to hear how versatile the actors are in terms of vocal age and accent range as well as how they connect imaginatively with the pieces.

Straight after these monologues, each actor reads a short piece of prose that has been given to them earlier that day. This tests their ability to lift lines from the page and make clear choices without having had much time to prepare.

There are four outright winners of this competition and the prize is a five-month binding contract with the BBC Radio Drama Company. There are also four runners-up who get offered a freelance contract for one radio drama project scheduled for that winter. The winners will not only be getting a job, but also the chance to work with established actors, writers and directors in a medium that they can extend their training in.

The Hobsons Prize

Hobsons is a large, well-established voice-over agency, which set up this competition in 2008 in order to promote voice-over work as a creative endeavour and also to discover new talent. There are up to four entrants from each accredited drama school. Each student submits a recording to the judges, who then select finalists to come in to a London recording studio and work in front of them on scripts from commercials that they have not seen previously. The prize is representation by the agency, a voice-reel and the chance to watch an established voice-over artist working. When you submit your recording, do not try to mimic someone else's voice and style; it is important that you discover your own. Judges will be looking for a voice that has a distinctive quality as well as for someone who understands the demands of a script, can take direction, and make choices quickly and professionally.

The Spotlight Prize

Each accredited drama school puts forward one third-year actor. This actor is supposedly the best in their year, although take this with a pinch of salt as being the best at acting can be hard to quantify! The students have three minutes each to impress an invited audience of about three hundred people from the industry: casting directors, agents, directors and actors. There is a panel of judges, who choose one outright winner and one highly commended runner-up. Judges commented that the performers who were able to relax tended to do better as they were able to be more honest, acting with their whole body rather than being stiff and locked in with tension. Relaxation allows personality to come through and the meaning of the speech to be conveyed to those watching. There is a cash prize for the winners, and for all the performers it is a fantastic opportunity to be seen in front of an audience of industry professionals. As the years have gone by, the evening has become increasingly glamorous and is an exciting event to be involved in.

Sam Wanamaker Festival

This is not a competition but an event that has been running since 2007 named after the American actor and director Sam Wanamaker, who founded Shakespeare's Globe based on the South Bank in London.

Forty-four students, two from each of the accredited drama schools, perform scenes by Shakespeare and his contemporaries on the Globe stage. They then all come together to dance a jig in front of the full house of spectators, comprising of about fifteen hundred people, many of whom will be agents and industry professionals. The performance is a culmination of a weekend of workshops, talks and rehearsals, where students will get help and advice from the Globe's voice, text and movement teachers, as well as from actors who have worked there. This is clearly a wonderful opportunity not only to be seen but also to have the experience of working on heightened text with experts in such an inspiring environment.

Independent Research Projects

Will I be expected to take on work of an academic nature in the third year?

If your course is an honours degree, then it is likely that you will be expected to engage in some research-based activity. This could take the form of a piece of written work, usually eight to ten thousand words long, that requires you to reflect on a topic related to your training, the subject of which you choose yourself. You will be required to show an ability to analyse and contextualise the ideas that your research looks into.

Some colleges allow you to do a practice-based project. You might write a play, or direct one, or you might make a short film. You could do a documentary about the ideas that you are examining. In other words, you will be offered the chance to show your powers of reflection and analysis through an alternative medium to writing. It is likely, however, that you will still need to submit a written component to accompany your practice-based research, but the amount you write will be limited.

Some schools ask you to engage in reflection and analysis, but within the context of a production you are working on. The research you undertake as an actor and the process you go through to realise the performance will be used as points of reference for reflection and analysis.

You are on a vocational acting course, and that is never forgotten. You will not, therefore, have the same academic demands made of you as you would if you were studying at a regular university and not at an accredited drama school. If you are taking an honours degree then you will need to show some level of intellectual rigour. More importantly, as an actor you will be expected to think, to evaluate, to research and to contextualise. Engaging in an independent research project in your final year encourages you to do all that. This project gives you the opportunity to find out more about the ideas, methodologies and practices that you find interesting. Rather than it being burdensome, many students enjoy the process of research. Just allow yourself enough time to do it properly; if you leave it till the last moment the whole experience becomes extremely stressful and the result unsatisfactory.

Life Planning

How can I make plans for a career that seems to rely so much on luck?

Luck does have influence over how your career is going to pan out after you leave drama school. Often you hear people say that they got such-and-such a job because they were in the right place at the right time, or because they knew someone involved. An actor once told me that a director gave him a job because he walked into the audition wearing a cap! Yes indeed, how do you prepare for stuff like that?

When you leave drama school, it isn't just your career that is beginning, but also your life outside of an institution. For many of you, you will have spent all your life from the age of four in school or college. You may be heading towards your first experience of having no timetable to map your week out, no classes to serve as a scaffold for your days, no fellow students to compare experiences with. There are, however, things that you can prepare for, just as there will be things that will take you by surprise.

You need to have a photograph, an up-to-date CV and a good cover letter. You need to research as much as you can. You should know who the artistic directors are of the theatres and companies that you want to work for. You should familiarise yourself with the names of influential casting directors. You should be going to theatre and films as much as you can, and have an opinion about what is going on in the industry. Don't wait until you leave to get involved in the world.

You should also ensure that you are as fit as you can possibly be and looking your best. Make sure you are drinking plenty of water, taking vitamins, getting sleep and exercise. You don't know when you might be called in for a casting, and you don't want to blow it by looking drained or unfit. You should not forget that you are about to enter a very competitive industry where looks feature large. It is not about being rake thin or having the appearance of a model – actors take many shapes and forms – but it is about looking well and energised. Your skin needs to be as clear as possible, and your body should be fit. Remember, don't try and look like some one else: look like you, just looking your best.

Before you leave drama school, make a list of all your capabilities. Some of these will be related to your chosen profession, some will not. You may well write down singing or tap-dancing, but equally you might add baking or swimming to your list. Think about what you love doing as well as what you are good at. Next year you are going to have to make a living between jobs – unless you are extremely lucky and get offered non-stop acting work – and it may be that you have skills that could earn you money and that you would enjoy using. If you have had some teaching experience, think about how you could exploit that to get work next year. Could you teach the piano or offer drama classes for kids? If you are good at magic tricks, for instance, lots of restaurants employ good magicians and people love a bit of magic at a party! If you make beautiful cakes, could you make money baking for birthdays and other occasions? I commissioned an actor recently to paint a portrait of my kids – she had had no formal training but she had always loved drawing and was good at it. The result was beautiful, and from it she has got a lot more work. When you leave college you will need to be available and ready for acting work, but life can get dispiriting if you find yourself temping five days a week, waiting for that call from your agent. Think ahead, what else are you good at? What other experience have you had? Now is the time to make some plans, because you are in the luxurious position of still being at college, rather than having to get a job immediately to pay the rent.

I haven't focused on acting a lot during this section, although that is, of course, what you will spend the bulk of your time doing. You will continue to develop as an actor throughout your third year, working on a variety of plays and with different directors. This gives you the opportunity to put into practice your training so far and to strengthen your understanding of your own process. The fact that you will get experience of working with a variety of directors is useful, as they will all make different demands on you and have different ways of approaching the text. You will need to be adaptable and be able to serve the director and the play in the knowledge that you have tools that will support you. Make sure that you build up good relationships with everyone you work with; you never know when they might be casting something that you are right for.

As a result of this final year of training, you will:

- Have developed as an actor, exploring a range of texts that place different demands on you.

- Have gained further experience of, and technique in, acting for camera.

- Have gained experience of radio work and learned microphone technique.

- Have a sense of the nature of your voice and its distinctive qualities.

- Have gained experience of audition and casting techniques.

- Have performed in front of an invited audience of industry professionals.

- Have been given a sense of the world that you are about to enter from visiting professionals.

- Be armed with a good headshot and CV.

Part Four:
Life After Drama School

Life After Drama School

When you think about the year ahead, you probably either feel terrified of the future, or nostalgic for the past. Ex-students tell me that they feel a mixture of relief, excitement, hope, terror and sadness, and a lot more besides – sometimes simultaneously! Hopefully you view your time at drama school in a positive light, and see it as a place which fostered your confidence and gave you tools to use in your work, and where you forged strong and lasting friendships. But nothing goes on for ever and you are now embarking on the career that you have been training for and anticipating for the last three years.

The aim of this final section is to provide you with some guidance as to what you can expect over the coming year, and how you can give yourself the best possible chance of succeeding. This is an unpredictable profession – you could be working in Pizza Hut one moment and in the new Tim Burton movie the next. You could face months out of work or hop from one job to another. I cannot possibly give you advice that covers every eventuality, but I hope that the information contained here proves useful. As in Part Three, this section is made up of frequently asked questions and answers that come from my many conversations with industry professionals.

Aims

- To offer advice concerning agents.

- To encourage you to market yourself.

- To offer you advice on auditioning.

- To provide you with practical information about the business.

- To help you to work out ways to make money between acting jobs.

- To encourage you to keep creatively fulfilled and in control of your life during potentially difficult times.

Agents

I left drama school without getting an agent, how do I go about getting one?

Although casting directors that I have spoken to say that they do sometimes call an actor who hasn't got representation in for an audition, it is important that you get yourself an agent. Agents make their living from the commission that you pay them when you get acting work, so they have an incentive to put you forward for auditions. They will have more contacts than you do and will be in regular dialogue with casting directors, directors and producers. They also know how to negotiate contracts. Having a good agent gives you more credibility in the business. As an actor just graduating from drama school you will probably feel more confident if there is someone else out there, other than your mother, fighting your corner!

Useful Websites

If you do not have representation, you need to make contact with people who can offer you work that you can then invite prospective agents to view. If you already have an agent, it is still important that you are proactive and work to get jobs for yourself. There are several resources that you can draw on in order to find out about auditions and castings.

Spotlight (www.spotlight.com)

This is an online site for performers and agents and casting directors. There is an annual subscription charge, which this year was £144 for established actors, but graduates leaving an accredited drama school are automatically invited to subscribe for half the full price. On leaving drama school your photograph should be listed here as well as your CV, and you can also post voice and video clips on the site. For performers without an agent, Spotlight forwards all casting enquiries that may come your way. Casting directors can view your details, actors and agents can find out what is being cast. It is a point of reference used by everyone in the business. It sends out job information and casting breakdowns, and also offers advice. Spotlight also provides you with lists of free workshops and talks, specifically aimed at graduates.

PCR Production Casting Report (www.pcrnewsletter.com/pcr)

Here you subscribe to a weekly online report containing up-to-date information about auditions for theatre, film and television. At the time of writing, this service costs you from £5.18 per week and provides you with casting breakdowns and contact details. You can find out about fringe productions, low-paid and unpaid acting work here too. The website also offers an email service alerting you to last-minute casting calls and auditions.

Casting Call Pro (www.castingcallpro.com/uk)

This is another online directory of professional actors, pre-senters, agents and casting directors. Through it you can list your profile, get information about castings, agents and photographers, as well as network with other members. You can only be a member if you have been to an accred-ited drama school or have done a minimum of three professional jobs (speaking parts not extra work). It doesn't cost you anything to list your profile on this site but there is a subscription for further services. The standard mem-bership, which is free, allows you to upload your CV, one photograph and one file, either a voice-over, or a showreel. These can be changed and there is no time limit for how long your profile can be on the site. You will not, however, be able to apply for paid jobs via the website, although you will be offered limited information on auditions that are happening and you can apply for unpaid work.

At the time of writing, the premium membership costs £20.40 per month, including VAT (or £156 a year, includ-ing VAT). The monthly contract is rolling and can be stopped at any time. As a premium member, you can upload twenty photographs and several other files. There is a template which you can use to create your own per-sonalised website. You are able to see who has checked into your profile, as well as information about which agents are looking for clients. You can apply for paid jobs via the website.

IdeasTap (www.ideastap.com)

This is an arts charity, which has been established to help young people at the start of their career. IdeasTap is not a social-network site, rather it provides an online forum for people to meet others in order to collaborate creatively, share ideas and pass on advice. It offers information about events, productions and exhibitions, as well as ideas about career development. Through it you can apply for funding for your own project, and you can advertise shows you are involved in. It is a free site aimed at creating a supportive and inspirational community for creative young people. You might join forces with others and collaborate in producing your own work, which you can then invite agents and casting directors to. There is also a jobs section on this site.

The Stage (www.thestage.co.uk)

The Stage is a newspaper that provides you with news about the industry and listings of auditions. There is an annual subscription charge to access it online, and if you pay yearly by direct debit, the fee is £53 at the time of writing. If you divide this into quarterly payments via direct debit, then the cost will be £14 every three months. If you are paying for your subscription using a credit or debit card then you will pay £58.50 for the year.

The British Theatre Guide
(www.britishtheatreguide.info)

This is a free website providing you with information about what's going on in the theatre, both amateur and professional, throughout the UK. You can find articles, listings of theatres, agents, actors and directors, news of forthcoming productions, and reviews of current shows. There is also a great glossary of theatrical terms listed here, which you might find very useful.

The UK Theatre Web (www.uktw.co.uk)

This site gives you information about what's on in the performing arts throughout the UK. You can find reviews, news about upcoming productions, details of venues and information about events and exhibitions. It also offers a comparison of ticket prices and their availability.

All of these sites are checked and regulated so you do not need to feel anxious about the legitimacy of anyone you are contacting.

Amongst other things, you should be applying for roles in plays going on in fringe theatre, which means you almost certainly won't be paid, so be careful to choose projects that are interesting and, wherever possible, original. Industry professionals will be much more likely to come and see something that looks vibrant and new than a tired old revamping of a play that has been done to death. If you are in something that gets good reviews or press releases, enclose those when you invite people to see the show.

When you are applying for a job, make sure you are specific in what you are suggesting yourself for. When you hear of a production you'd like to go up for, wait until a casting director has been named before you send off your details, unless you know the director involved. Pick roles that you genuinely think you are appropriate for. Find out about the production or the company and suggest good reasons why you should be considered for the role. You must sell yourself in any covering letter.

Marketing Yourself

How do I know how to market myself when I have played such a broad range of roles at drama school?

Sometimes it can be confusing for an actor straight from drama school to know how they might be viewed by a casting director, and the sort of roles that they might be seen for. With this in mind, answer these questions:

- What type of role have you been most successful in?

- What type of role do you really struggle to engage with?

- What roles do you enjoy playing?

- What sorts of projects excite you?

- If you were a casting director, realistically how would you cast yourself?

- Very specifically, what is it that you would like from your career?

- What is your 'USP', or unique selling point? In other words, what do you have that other actors do not?

- What is your build?

- Where are you from?

- Do you play an instrument?

- Do you look particularly young or older than your age?

Considering these questions, and others like them, you can start to see where you are comfortable being cast, where you would like to be cast and how others who are responsible for casting might view you. In order to help you understand this last point more fully, start paying close attention to the different kinds of roles that you see both in theatre and in television.

Often in television, when it comes to types of character, there are broader generalisations than there are in theatre. Make a list of the different types that crop up regularly. For example:

- Banker

- Mistress

- Thug

- Innocent

- Young parent

- Villain

- Soldier

- Doctor

- Teacher

- Psychopath

- Hippy

- Geek

- Loyal friend

- Tramp

- Classy

- Working class

- Social worker

- Clown

- Motherly

- Clean cut

- Lawyer

- Prostitute

There are many more that you can add. Now look through your list and see what you might be cast as. I am certainly not advocating that you settle for a reductive process of typecasting, but you do need to market yourself, and that involves understanding how you might be placed in a world that does often require you to be categorised in some way.

Student Films

Doing student films is a great way of getting experience, making contacts for the future and also of boosting the credits on your CV in an otherwise lean period. Film schools regularly advertise for actors to work with their students, but be careful: make sure that the project involves final-year or MA students. An actor I spoke to discovered that, when he worked with less-experienced students, some of them were still struggling to work out how to take the lens cap off! If you want to use some of the material from the film to show to an agent or to edit into a showreel, get permission in writing from the film-makers before you send off any clips.

Equity (www.equity.org.uk)

Equity is the UK trade union for professional performers and creative practitioners. In the past you had to be a member of Equity in order to work professionally – it was very difficult for actors to work without getting an Equity card, and it was very difficult to get an Equity card without work! That little card signifying that you were a member of the union was highly prized. Now you no longer have to be a member of Equity to get acting work, but it is a very good idea to join. As individuals, actors don't have a whole lot of power, but they gain strength in numbers. Equity operates to improve your working conditions, maintain your legal rights, negotiate on your behalf over pay levels and hours, check health-and-safety issues, provide accommodation lists, offer careers advice and operate a pension scheme. You never know when you might need help. An actor friend of mine had an accident onstage a while ago. Her costume was too long and, although she had brought this to the attention of the company, nothing had been done about it. One night she tripped on her trouser leg and fell, breaking her foot in the process. The result was she could not continue with the job and was out of work for an extended period. Through Equity she filed for compensation and so was able to pay her rent during this difficult time. This is just one example – joining the union could be beneficial to you too.

Castings

I have a casting for a commercial, what should I expect?

You will find that you get quite used to showing up for commercial castings. Often your agent will phone the night before for a casting the next morning. When you arrive, you will usually find a lot of actors waiting to be seen. The sessions are generally quite brief: you simply need to go in and do whatever it is that is required very quickly. Immediate results are needed, and often the company that has arranged the casting won't know quite what it is they are looking for to sell their brand until they see it.

Once in the room, you will be asked for your name and what you have been up to lately. The casting director will ask you to show your hands back and front and to turn each way in profile for the camera. You will then, more often than not, be asked to engage in an imaginary task such as eating some very gorgeous yogurt or looking pleased because your children have been protected from germs in the toilet. There will in fact be no yogurt and no clean children, so you need to be able to create the scenario for yourself! An ex-student of mine told me that nothing could have prepared him for commercial castings, given the things that he had been asked to do over the past few months – such as saying 'No, thanks!' to a mouse that was offering him half a mince pie, kiss a wall, make breakfast for a vast family, build a car out of cardboard boxes, chat up a horse, dance in a supermarket, fold up a television, drive countless cars and two boats, fly a helicopter and run through a forest whilst eating a biscuit.

If you get cast in a commercial, it can be very lucrative, so it is well worth your time going to the castings. Dress in a way that is appropriate for the role – if you need guidance on this start watching adverts closely, noting the different 'types' that are used to sell products. It is a good idea to have a couple of outfits ready so you don't have to agonise too much every time about what to wear. If you find that you are being called in a lot to try out for the 'young mum' role or the 'smart-casual best mate', think what clothes are appropriate and keep them ready. Always be on time and be friendly and upbeat. You will probably go to many castings, but actually get very few of them. That is quite normal. Be prepared, but don't take it all too seriously. Not getting a job on a commercial is no reflection of your talent. If you have the time, it is a good idea to fix up an appointment to see a friend or do something interesting after your casting, like going to a gallery or a film. That way it feels as if you are just stopping off somewhere to do a quick job before getting on with the main thrust of your day. I say this because actors can become depressed after a while when they find themselves attending a great many of these commercial castings with little success.

I have a casting for a West End musical, what should I expect?

Generally, as a starting point, you will need two songs – one uptempo and one ballad – to show your range. You may also have been asked for something more specific, like a rock song or a comedy song. At the audition, make sure that you give the pianist accompanying you music that is easy to read. It should be in a folder or taped together, and it should be in your key. If at all possible, try to have at least one coaching session prior to the audition to ensure that you really know the songs. Usually you sing first, and then if you have been successful you will be recalled for a dance call, where you will have to pick up a routine with other people who have been called back. The standard of dancing that is required of you will depend on how much you will be asked to do in the show. The dancing can be quite gruelling, so you need to make sure you are in good shape. If you get the job, you may find yourself doing eight shows a week, so the people auditioning you not only need to see that you have ability, but that you have stamina too. If you are successful, you may be called back for several rounds of auditions before any final casting decisions are made. You really need to have a very good singing voice and be able to pick up dance routines quickly and easily to get through the rounds of auditions. It is a brutal and exacting process.

How long before the audition do I get the script for television?

This varies. For a soap audition, you often first see the script on the day of the casting itself, so it really pays to arrive early and give yourself a chance to read it through and break it down. This is not always the case, but certainly you can expect to get scripts at the last minute.

For other television drama you may have longer with the script – as much as a week, but on average a few days. It's possible that you have been called in to read for one part but have then been asked to look at another, and given ten minutes to read over the new scenes. If this happens, you should take it in your stride and enjoy it because it is an indicator that the director likes you. When reading through the new scene, you should trust your first instincts and go with them.

It is unlikely that you will be sent the whole script, but rather selected scenes from it. These may be referred to as 'sides'. However long you have with the script, make sure that you read it all, not just your lines within it. You will be expected to have a sense of the journey of the scene and your relationships to the other characters involved. Whether you have two weeks to prepare or one night, it is your job to be ready for the casting. You will need to be absolutely familiar with the script, have thought what the scene is about and have made choices to bring into the audition with you.

Should I learn the lines for an audition?

Most people that I have spoken to, actors and casting directors alike, think that wherever possible this is a good idea. Apart from anything else, it means that you won't be fussing with pages in the audition and that you will be able to look up, listen to the lines coming from the other characters and make choices unencumbered by the physical necessity of locating your lines on the page. A writer who has just been involved in casting her work for a major new television drama said that every actor that came to audition had learnt their lines. Quite simply, it is your job to be absolutely prepared, and even if you get emailed the scenes the night before you should attempt to learn them. It doesn't really matter if you forget your lines from time to time and have to glance down at the script; what matters is that you come into the room confident and in a position to make choices and take any direction you are offered. In this way, the script comes to life and those responsible for casting can really *see* you in the role – learning your lines gives you the best chance to do this. An actor I spoke to said that at the last film casting he went to, even though he had a lot of scenes and relatively little time to learn them in, it was clear when he arrived at the audition that the expectation was that he would know his words. This is not about being absolutely word perfect, this is about bringing the part to life and giving the director a chance to see what you are capable of without the barrier of a script in the way. There are a lot of actors out there, so you have to give yourself the best possible chance in every casting. Obviously, if you only get the script on the day, it may not be possible to learn your lines. In this situation at least make sure that you are as familiar as possible with them. If you do forget the words or get in a muddle, don't apologise, come out of character and make a big deal out of it. Keep calm, figure out where you are, and carry on. If you feel that you absolutely haven't done yourself justice, you can always ask to read again: the worst that can happen is that they say no.

Should I dress as the part for a TV casting?

It is a good idea to dress in something indicative of the character without going to extremes. If the part is glamorous then you should look glamorous; if you're up for a banker, a suit might be appropriate. A casting director I spoke to said that she was once casting a television drama involving a gang of mods, and everyone auditioning showed up in a parka. She said it really helped the director to visualise the actors in the role. Make sure your hair is appropriate too: if you are up for the part of a soldier, your shoulder-length curls might have to be trimmed a little! There is no need to go overboard, but you can certainly help the director imagine you in the role with what you are wearing.

I am dyslexic and worried about sight-reading. What should I do?

A surprising amount of actors are dyslexic so you should not panic, you are in good company. You will need to develop your own strategy that works best for you. I am sure that you already have devices in place to help you with reading in an audition situation. If it is at all possible, get to any audition early so that, if you haven't been sent the script before, you will have time to go through it before meeting the casting director. Annotate it in any way that is useful to you. One actor I knew used to draw images for every line of text; this was something that helped him. You may find you don't have time to work like this, or it may simply not serve you. If you are asked to sight-read, there is nothing wrong with telling the director that you are dyslexic. Don't apologise for it. It is simply information that you may need to pass on. Remember, stuttering over a word or getting lines the wrong way round is really not an issue in an audition. Reading perfectly is not an indication of a good actor. The director will be looking for your intentions, your responses, the choices you make, the way you interact. Forget about being fantastic at sight-reading and go back to thinking about what the scene is asking of you as an actor.

If you have absolutely no time to look the scene over, then just take a little chunk at a time to break down the line. So, for example, if the text reads:

> I can't believe it you came all this way on your own just to see me and I wasn't even there.

You might break it down like this:

> I can't believe it / you came all this way / on your own / just to see me / and I wasn't even there.

It doesn't matter how you break it down, the point is you are committing to one moment in the text at a time, and not trying to tackle the whole thing at once. Look up, deliver a small section of the text, make a choice with it, finish the thought, and then look down to get your next little chunk of words.

Will I need to do monologues for a theatre audition?

All directors are different and will ask different things of you. Some will get you to improvise, some will get you to read from the play you are auditioning for, some will ask for monologues. Before you go to a meeting, you should be told what will be required of you. That said, it is quite rare now to be asked to perform monologues at an audition, although you should always have a classical and contemporary speech prepared just in case. An exception is auditioning for companies involved in theatre-in-education (TIE) and for the RSC, both of which often ask for monologues. TIE is thriving, and auditions for this area of work will be listed on the websites that I mentioned earlier.

A writer whose work is put on regularly at theatres such as the Royal Court and the National, and is heavily involved in the casting of his plays, told me that he is fascinated sitting in on auditions as it is often the first time he hears extracts from his plays aloud in any way. Hearing actors read and be directed on that reading allows him to gain a fresh understanding of his own work and the director's work. This is the power that you have as an actor: you get to bring the text to life, and that is what will be expected of you at an audition.

In order to bring that text to life, just as with a casting for television, you will be required to be absolutely prepared. That will mean at the very least being extremely familiar with the scenes that you will be reading at the audition. This familiarity does not simply mean knowing your words and what is happening to your character, but involves you thinking about the play as a whole. You should think about the story, the characters and the structure of the whole piece. You should think about how the play affects you emotionally and intellectually. You should have questions ready about anything you don't understand or want more information on. Again, even if you get details of the audition only the day before, it is your job to have read the whole play and to have an opinion about it. A director I spoke to said that he asked actors to leave if they hadn't read the whole of the play that they were auditioning for. Having prepared well, in the audition itself you need to be open and engage with the director's notes, flexible enough to try out new ideas.

On the rare occasions when you are asked to prepare a monologue, again make sure that you have read the whole play that it comes from. Don't just buy one of those books of monologues for actors and learn a speech that you like. You need to have an understanding of the function of your character and the arc of their journey throughout the play. Remember, there are thousands of actors – what is going to mark you out as someone that the director wants to work with?

Audition Technique

How can I improve my audition technique?

Whether you are auditioning for theatre, film or television, relaxation is key. One casting director I spoke to made the point that if you are called in for an audition, that alone should boost your confidence. There are thousands of actors listed in Spotlight who have not been considered for the part, but the director has asked to see you because she thinks that you can act and might be right for the role. The director is not there to criticise you or judge you, but to cast you. You have to believe that it is well within your grasp to get the job. Think about those tennis matches you have seen played out at Wimbledon: at a certain level it is often the player who believes he is going to win that actually does so in the end. When his opponent gets tense and blows a match point, he stays focused and calm, making those winning shots.

Preparation will help raise your confidence levels. Read the whole script, or as much of it as you have been sent, several times. If it is from a published play, get hold of the script and read it all. Think what the scenes that you are reading are about: how are the characters relating to each other? Break down your scenes further. What has your character been doing just before the scene starts? What does your character want in the scene? How does your character go about getting what he wants? Look closely at where the arc of the scene falls: is there a pivotal moment, which your scene builds towards and then afterwards deals with? As you read, make strong choices. When you get into the audition room, you can always ask the director how far they would like you to go with an idea, but make sure you are prepared to make offers and try things out. Learn the lines if you have any opportunity to do so and if it is appropriate.

If you are auditioning for a soap opera, make sure that you have considered its distinctive style. Find out about the director of the film or play you are up for, what sort of work has he or she done in the past? Does the company you are auditioning for have any particular ethos or way of working that it might help you to know about?

Ask yourself before you go to the audition how you might come across in a casting. I talked before about the ways that we can let ourselves down when we are nervous. Do your insecurities show when you meet casting directors and directors? Think about your body language.

Do you always make eye contact? Do you smile when you meet people for the first time? Do you come across as the sort of person someone might want to work with? This is crucial. Everyone I spoke to said that you should not come to the audition at all unless you are able to communicate your desire to be there and your commitment to playing this specific role. That doesn't mean you need to gush about how wonderful the experience would be, rather that you make sure that you are present in and engaged with the audition, and in any ideas about the play that might come up. Do not present yourself as someone who is just looking in on this audition before rushing off to another appointment, or as someone so cool that they cannot sit upright in their chair! Remember, not only is the director casting a role but they are also looking to employ a member of a company, and this might involve spending months with that actor. You need to look as though you are up for the ride! Bear in mind too that all these industry professionals talk to each other – if you come across well in an audition, even if you don't get the job, this will be noted and may well result in more castings further down the line. Conversely, not engaging fully in an audition can also cause the director to go off you permanently, and to discourage others from employing you.

Never ever be late for an audition. Not only will running late make you feel unbelievably stressed, but it will also do you no favours whatsoever in the eyes of those casting. They won't really be interested in excuses, and although they might listen quite politely this will be down to good manners rather than any genuine sympathy. They have a schedule, and it is your job to keep to your part of it. If you can't arrive on time to an audition, how can you be relied on to get to the film set or rehearsal room at the appointed hour? Give yourself much more time than you think it will take to get to your meeting. Allow for potential train delays and traffic jams and being unable to find the address. You can always go for a coffee and go over your script if you get there too early.

Take your time before you start the audition. It may well be that you will be asked to read with the casting director, particularly in the early stages of casting. Make sure that you do not pick up on their rhythms. They are not an actor so be prepared to get little from them in that department. If you are holding a script, check that it is not obscuring your face, but equally do not put it on the table in front of you so that you will be obliged to keep looking down at it. Hold it at chest height. Keep your thumb on the page as a marker of where you are up to in the script.

When sight-reading, take one little chunk of text at a time and don't attempt to absorb more than that in one go. Make sure that you have made a choice as to how to play that small section and look up to speak the lines. Keep eye contact until the end of the thought. Don't look back at the script until that thought has landed and you have received anything that might come back at you. You may not feel that it is appropriate for your character to look continually at the person they are speaking to. Obviously people look away at times during conversation, sometimes to get a thought, recall a memory or because they feel uncomfortable or distracted. This is fine, just don't keep your face buried in the script, and if you have space to move around in a theatre audition, don't turn your back or position yourself in profile for too long. You are interesting, but the director needs to be able to see you to establish that!

Do not be tempted to look back down at the script as soon as you have finished your bit to see what lines you have next. It is not about getting the lines right, it is about your performance, and that includes listening and responding as well as talking, so make sure that you stay connected to the person speaking. Try to really hear what they are saying; it is all too easy to start anticipating your next moment before you have dealt with the moment you are in, and that means you stop listening. *How* you listen to whoever it is you are reading with is crucially important. A director will be focusing on this as much as on how you speak the text. He will want to see your reactions, particularly on camera. He may even ask you to do a scene that has no speaking in it, where you open a letter containing sad news for example, or poke your head round a door to see if anyone is there. Keep breathing throughout the scene. A new thought will have a new breath; connect to it, and it will keep what you are doing specific and help you to stay relaxed.

If you are asked to improvise, get straight to the heart of what is going on in the scene, don't pad things out with unnecessary talk. Never try to outdo your fellow improvisers. It is not about being the funniest or most emotional or saying the most things. The purpose is to see how open you are, how you work with other people and how well you have understood your character and the scene.

After you have read, never apologise for it going badly or criticise what you did. You mustn't show dislike for your performance. You don't know how it was received by the people auditioning you, and if you look as if you don't believe in yourself, how can you expect them to? If you fluff a line or turn over two pages of the script at once, don't make a big deal out of it. People do stutter over words from time to time and the director is not looking for someone who turns pages well; keep your focus on what is happening for the character.

You can improve your sight-reading technique by constantly reading aloud at home. There are also workshops that you can go to that are advertised on the websites that I mentioned earlier. Some of these are very expensive, but people who have attended classes of this nature report that even the cheaper ones are very useful too.

Learning Lines

The mark of a good actor is not whether you find learning lines easy or not – like most things some people are better at it than others. Your starting point should never be to learn your lines by rote. If you explore the scene itself, and its context within the play, you will find that you naturally begin to remember your lines because your brain, having understood the purpose of the dialogue, will latch on to it more easily. Think *why* your character says what he or she does. What has just been happening? What are they trying to get from those around them? *How* are they trying to get it? As you rehearse, *actually* listen to those you are working with; your line is a response to what is happening to your character. In isolation, the words are meaningless, as a response to somebody or something outside of yourself they become relevant and so are absorbed more quickly. When you are going over your lines, never try and memorise *how* to play a line, the *how* comes in the playing of the scene with the other actors.

People offer all sorts of strategies to assist line-learning and you will get to know what works best for you. Here are some popular methods, but remember learning lines is not the starting point, getting to understand the text and your character is:

- Going over the scene with someone else. Your partner will have the text and will prompt you if you lose your way. It will make the process of learning your lines easier if you have someone to respond to.

- Make a recording of each scene. You can do this by taping everyone else's lines and leaving gaps in the recording where your own lines come in. Or you can simply record all the lines, and through the repetition of listening, memorise them. There is a useful app that you can download called LineLearner by AlldayApps. It costs £2.49, and is recommended by actors.

- Visualise what you are saying. For example, if you are talking about certain people, put a face to each person you mention. If you are describing a particular place, make sure you can picture it in your mind's eye; the colours, the shapes, etc. If you have a rather dry list of scientific symbols, then give each of these a separate image that brings them to life for you. Some actors find it useful to draw the images. It is often easier to remember things when you can visualise them.

- Write the lines down by hand. The physical action of committing your lines to paper may help you to remember them more easily.

- Move about. Sometimes if you are sitting very still trying to focus on committing something to memory, your mind becomes locked and unresponsive. Try moving as you go over your lines. Associate the words with corresponding physical actions. For example, if my line is 'It's not fair', then perhaps I will stamp my feet or throw a cushion against a wall. If my line is 'I will make sure everyone knows about this', I might point my finger aggressively, jabbing it in the air. By linking the physical with the cerebral, you may find that the words are absorbed more effortlessly.

- Keep reading the whole play through.

- Use mnemonics. These are simply strategies for improving your memory and they come in several forms, many of which you will already be familiar with. They rely on associations between something that you find easy to remember, and the word that you are trying to memorise. You will, for example, probably have heard the mnemonic commonly used to help people remember the colours of the rainbow. It is an acronym, where the word is replaced with another beginning with the same first letter: Red, Orange, Yellow, Green, Blue, Indigo, Violet becomes Richard Of York Gave Battle In Vain. A code I needed to remember was 2708b. For some reason it wouldn't sink in, but I associated the number '27' with a particular film and came up with the sentence, '*27 Dresses*, oh 8, brilliant!' – I no longer forgot the code! As you can see from this, mnemonics do not have to be logical. They can be useful devices to use if you have long lists to remember, perhaps involving convoluted explanations, or scientific or medical terms.

What to Do When You Can't Get Acting Work

Putting on your own show

A lot of actors are very proactive and create work for themselves, which is great in terms of keeping creatively fulfilled and also for producing things that you can invite people from the industry to come and see. It is, though, a serious undertaking and involves a great many factors that you may not be aware of in your initial enthusiasm to put a show on. Not only is there a lot of work involved, but you should never underestimate the cost of putting on a production, even on a very small scale. You should not be deterred, however, if you are passionate about a piece. Ex-students have formed successful companies. The Edinburgh Festival Fringe, which takes place every August, for example, is bulging with shows that have been put on by people fresh out of drama school. You need to do your research – passion is a wonderful thing, but it needs to be accompanied by pragmatism. There are two very useful books that you should read as a starting point: *So You Want To Do A Solo Show?* and *So You Want To Be A Theatre Producer?* Details of both of these can be found at the back of this book.

What can I do to keep myself alive creatively when I am unemployed?

It is so important that you keep yourself stimulated and challenged in-between acting jobs. Not only will you feel happier as a result, but you will also have something to talk about the next time you get an audition. If you do nothing but work in a call centre and wait for your agent to ring, then you are not engaging in life, and that is such a waste.

See as much theatre and film as you possibly can. You need to know what is going on in your profession and you need to keep your passion for acting alight. Most theatres offer discounts for students or under-twenty-fives, and previews are often cheaper.

Read classic novels. They will fuel your imagination and give you a broader context of the world and its history.

Listen to music, even music that you might find difficult or that you don't immediately engage with.

Go to galleries. Stimulate your imagination visually by looking at the work of artists that you may never even have heard of before. Consider why a painting moves you, or leaves you unaffected.

Sit in cafés and watch people pass, observe how they move, note down their rhythms and mannerisms, how they engage with each other. Spend one day a week adopting the persona of someone you have been watching. Make up a backstory for them, how might they sit, dress, eat. What do they carry in their bag?

Read plays. If you are ignorant of a particular genre, focus on that. Make sure you have also read lots of new writing and know the nature of the plays that are being written today and where they are being put on. You could form a play-reading group with other actors.

If you like writing then explore it further. A playwright I spoke to said that an actor should write the play that they always dreamed would be written for them. They should make it as rigorous and as active, as well-structured and well-wrought as they dreamed that play would be. If you feel that you can't quite write a play or a novel yet, then just keep a journal of your observations, thoughts and ideas.

If you can sing or play an instrument then join a choir, a band or an orchestra. If you haven't got the time to commit fully to something like a choir, then at least get involved with other people who might want to sing or play with you in a less formal capacity.

Go to classes. There are plenty going on. Look at the Actors Centre for information on a range of classes and workshops (www.actorscentre.co.uk). IdeasTap (www.ideastap.com) also has information about events, as do the other websites I mentioned earlier. The Actors' Temple offer classes specifically on the Meisner Technique (www.actorstemple.com). Keep working on your voice and body, keep going to classes that stimulate your imagination. American actors never stop going to classes, it is only in this country we think that, once we have finished our training, we are done. Some of the classes are more expensive than others, but there are always things going on that don't cost a great deal of money.

Whatever you do, don't do nothing. Time passes very quickly and you don't want to look back in years to come and take stock of all the time you wasted waiting for the phone to ring, when you could have been out there challenging and educating yourself. In short, having a life!

How can I make money between jobs?

You have to be able to pay your rent and eat, and unless you get very well-paid acting work that can tide you over between jobs, it is more than likely that you will have to find some sort of other employment to keep you afloat financially. The problem is that whatever work you do has to be flexible so that you are free to go to auditions, sometimes at short notice.

Actors often do shifts in bars and restaurants, because this involves working in the evenings when it is unlikely you will be called in for a casting. Daytime shifts can also be swapped around if the need arises. The pay is minimal, but this is boosted by what you receive in tips. As part of the deal you sometimes get a free meal too, so it is a handy way of getting your food for nothing. Try and find a restaurant that has a good atmosphere that you might enjoy working in, and obviously good restaurants will provide you with good meals. Living off a diet of burgers and chips might not be conducive to keeping in shape – and you need to keep yourself looking as fit and well as possible.

Actors very often join a temping agency, again because the hours are flexible. There are plenty of these to sign up to and, depending what it is, the work can be quite interesting. You will get to meet new people in different environments.

Working as an usher or in a theatre box office means that, although it is not hugely well paid, you will get to watch the shows going on in that theatre. You will also be part of a stimulating environment. As your colleagues will most likely also be performers of one sort or another, they will be sympathetic to your need to trade hours when auditions come through. You could start by contacting your local theatre to see if there is any work available there.

Actors find work as demonstrators in department stores, supermarkets and other retail businesses. You may have to display the stock, demonstrate how a product works and talk to passers-by about the product in order to increase its sales. It is useful work to pick up as you do not have to commit to it full-time, but can work single days and so keep yourself free for auditions when necessary. Jobs are advertised in Jobcentre Plus offices, local newspapers, recruitment agencies and individual employer's websites.

Information about working as an extra can be found in *Contacts* published by Spotlight (www.spotlight.com/shop). This work can be very dull, and involve long days with a lot of waiting around; however, it is relatively well paid. It will also give you a further understanding of how a television or film set operates.

There is a lot of work for actors in the corporate market, and this is generally well paid. If you look on the internet, there are several companies that employ actors for work in the corporate sector. Some useful websites to use as a starting point are:

- www.castingcallpro.com/uk

- www.corporateroleplay.co.uk

- www.roleplayreactors.co.uk

Do ensure you do some thorough research, find out what the different companies are looking for from an actor, and only send your CV off where you think it might be appropriate. It is also a good thing to talk to other actors who have been in the business for a while to see what contacts they might have that they can pass on to you.

Teaching is a really rewarding way of making money. Do you play an instrument well? Could you offer piano lessons or trombone tuition? You need to ask around, perhaps a parent or teacher you know could put up a sign in the local school or pass your name on to a friend who is looking. There are community websites (often based on postcodes) that act exactly like the old boards in newsagents. These are cheap or free to advertise on. You could also set up your own website to promote your skills.

Are there drama groups in your area, which might employ actors to teach children and young people? I have given several references in the past for actors wanting to teach, so I know that there are companies operating nationwide, which provide drama classes. Their turnover of teachers is high as people come and go to take on acting work. You could start by looking at the following websites:

- www.perform.org.uk

- www.stagecoach.co.uk

- www.dramaclasses.biz

If you do teach children, you will need to be CRB checked. This is a straightforward process during which your criminal record will be checked, and your suitability to work with children ascertained.

Are you a good dancer? Could you offer classes at your local community centre?

Have you thought about going into hospitals and reading to patients? An actor friend of mine regularly reads poetry to people who have suffered a stroke. It isn't hugely well paid but you do make some money and you also get to feel that you are putting your talents to very good use. Interact reading service employs professional actors to read to people who have had a stroke (www.interactreading.org). Not all actors are suitable for this sort of work, so you should expect a thorough interview followed by training before being offered a job.

Are you a good singer or do you play a musical instrument well? Could you get a band together and make money playing at weddings and other events?

Try to use your talents and build up contacts that can offer you work when acting jobs are thin on the ground. You don't want to spend your life in a call centre so think what it is that you have to offer that can make you money and that might also bring you some satisfaction. It may be that you have a skill that isn't specifically related to acting. You might bake the most beautiful cakes or make lovely cards or be a fantastic gardener.

Consider all your skills and resources; you don't have to be chained to a desk day in and day out when you are not acting. Ask other actors how they make a living between acting jobs, this way you can find out about opportunities and get details of new contacts.

Surviving Hard Times

How do I cope with rejection?

Being rejected is part of being an actor. This is tough, everyone seeks love and approval (and I think actors are particularly in need of both!), but you have to accept that rejection is part of your life now. Statistically, the more auditions you go to, the more likely you are to get a job. So for every 'no' you get, put a big tick by it because that is one rejection out of the way moving you closer to that all-important 'yes!' It is a bit like giving birth – each agonising contraction suffered moves you closer to the end of the pain and the joy of the new life.

So do not get weighed down by the seemingly endless cycle of audition and rejection. Think instead quite practically about why you didn't get the part. You will not get feedback from those auditioning you, but you can learn something by looking at whoever *did* get cast in the role. This can be a consolation because that person may well turn out to be a completely different age or type from you: the casting was not necessarily based on your acting but on the way that you looked. Perhaps on reflection you come to the conclusion, for example, that you needed to be better prepared, or less defensive. You should continue to be proactive, working on the problem rather than being defeated by it. One agent that I spoke to suggested that it was a good idea to keep a record of everything that you have been up for and how it went. You can look over it and see any patterns that might be emerging, helping you to pinpoint the problem. It is also a good idea to keep a diary like this so that you can remember directors and casting directors that you might want to contact in the future, particularly if the audition went well.

Carry on with classes, going to the theatre, seeing good films, reading great novels. Write, play music, go dancing; don't just sit and wait by the phone. Challenge and stimulate yourself.

Sir Richard Eyre, who has worked with some of the greatest actors in this country, said that you should 'be ambitious to be good, not to be successful or famous or rich', and that the qualities you will need to survive in this career other than talent, are 'patience and the ability to withstand disappointment'.[5] I hope that this helps get you through those darker hours when becoming an actor seems impossible.

By the end of this year I hope that:

- You are doing interesting rewarding work.

- That you have a greater sense of yourself and the profession that you have entered.

- That you have found ways of making money between acting jobs that do not plunge you into utter depression or boredom.

- That you are making use of all your talents and feeding your creativity even when your agent hasn't phoned for a while.

- That you remember that an artist aims to create something beautiful or meaningful in every piece of work they undertake. You can produce work of great worth regardless of how high profile the project is. Take pride in everything that you do.

Appendices

Further Reading 266

Bibliography of Plays Used 271

Endnotes 272

Further Reading

Bella Merlin, *Beyond Stanislavsky – The Psycho-physical Approach to Actor Training* (Nick Hern Books, 2001)
This is an inspirational book, written from the perspective of someone who has trained at Moscow's State Institute of Cinematography. Merlin provides an honest and accessible account of her experiences, outlining the struggles as well as the moments of exaltation. This is an important book to read in order to gain a deeper understanding of Stanislavsky's system in relation to your own work.

Bella Merlin, *The Complete Stanislavsky Toolkit* (Nick Hern Books, 2007)
This is a useful book because it outlines Stanislavsky's ideas in a practical way. I often use it as a source for exercises. It will refer you to key terms and vocabulary and is an essential point of reference.

Konstantin Stanislavski, (trans.) Jean Benedetti, *An Actor's Work* (Routledge, 2008)
Konstantin Stanislavski, (trans.) Jean Benedetti, *My Life in Art* (Routledge, 2008)
Konstantin Stanislavski, (trans.) Jean Benedetti, *An Actor's Work on a Role* (Routledge, 2010)
These books provide you with a really accessible insight into Stanislavsky's work and vision. They are both practical and inspirational. Jean Benedetti's translations are enjoyable reads in themselves, but they are also reminders of what it is to be an actor, and an artist.

Sanford Meisner and Dennis Longwell, *Sanford Meisner on Acting* (Vintage, 1987)
This is such a clear and easy book to read. It takes you through fifteen months' worth of Meisner's acting classes, following the progress of a particular group of students. Not only will you be reassured by the struggles that these actors face, but you will also get a sense of Sanford Meisner himself; his teaching methods, his passion and his personality.

Mike Alfreds, *Different Every Night – Freeing the Actor* (Nick Hern Books, 2007)
This book offers both actors and directors guidance through the process of preparing for a play, rehearsing it and performing it. I am often asked how an actor manages to invest their work with life throughout a long run of a production, and this book addresses that question. Alfreds gives you practical advice, and clearly outlines the purpose behind his ideas in a way that is reassuringly tangible.

Declan Donnellan, *The Actor and the Target* (Nick Hern Books, 2002; new edition, 2005)
This is a beautifully written and accessible book. It deals with those moments, recognised by all actors, when they simply don't know what to do, when they are blocked with fear and self-consciousness. Donnellan offers practical suggestions, guidance and instruction, but he does so in a way that is inspirational and thought-provoking.

Harold Guskin, *How to Stop Acting* (Methuen, 2004)
This book offers a strategy for auditioning, rehearsal and performance. It explores a simple but very useful concept about the way an actor can work in response to a text, rather than through imposing preconceived ideas onto it.

Alison Hodge (ed.), *Twentieth-Century Actor Training* (Routledge, 2000)
This book provides you with accounts of specific training exercises and the ideas behind them. It looks at the key principles of fourteen of the greatest twentieth-century theatre practitioners, and how those principles have been applied to productions. It will give you a great sense of the way actor training has developed over the years in the West, and you will be able to cross reference and compare methodologies. You may discover practitioners that you will not look at in any detail at drama school, but which might in time influence your work.

Cicely Berry, *Text in Action* (Virgin Books, 2001)
This book focuses primarily on Shakespeare, but Berry's techniques can be used for modern texts too. It addresses the key question of how to bring a play alive through the use of its language. The exercises are extremely useful in this book, as are the discussions that contextualise them. It is an absolutely essential read for anyone contemplating working on a classical text.

Mel Churcher, *Acting for Film* (Virgin Books, 2003)
This is such a useful book. It covers advice about the
casting process, auditioning, on-camera techniques, the
way a shoot is scheduled and ordered, how to cope with
being on a set for the first time, an outline of the
working environment of a film set, as well as exercises
and tips to do with acting and vocal issues. It deals with
a comprehensive range of factors that you will need to
know about if you want to work in films, and it does so
in a way that is direct and pragmatic

Andrew Tidmarsh and Tara Swart, *An Attitude for
Acting: How to Survive (and Thrive) as an Actor*
(Nick Hern Books, 2011)
This book encourages you to be proactive in getting
acting work, and offers guidance and advice about how
to go about this. There are practical exercises to help
you, as well as suggested techniques. The book covers
issues such as keeping motivated, preparing for
auditions, dealing with nerves, coping with rejection,
and developing your confidence.

James Seabright, *So You Want To Be A Theatre
Producer?* (Nick Hern Books, 2010)
This is a really useful resource for anyone thinking of
putting on their own show. It goes through every stage
of the process: developing an idea, raising money and
budgeting, negotiating rights, marketing the show,
finding a venue. It also provides lists of key press
contacts and rehearsal spaces.

Gareth Armstrong, *So You Want To Do A Solo Show?* (Nick Hern Books, 2011)
Again, this is a very useful resource for anyone thinking of putting on their own work. It covers everything you need to know, such as budgeting and marketing and finding a venue, but it also offers case studies from solo shows that have been successful so that you can get a tangible sense of how it all works.

Bibliography of Plays

Anton Chekhov, *The Cherry Orchard*, *Three Sisters* and *Uncle Vanya*, translated by Stephen Mulrine (Nick Hern Books, 1998, 1994, 1999, respectively)

Arthur Miller, *The Crucible* (Penguin Books, new edition, 2000). Copyright © Arthur Miller, 1952, 1953, 1954; copyright renewed © Arthur Miller, 1980, 1981, 1982. All rights reserved. Reproduced by permission of The Wylie Agency

Harold Pinter, *The Homecoming* (Faber and Faber, new edition 1991). Reproduced by permission of Faber and Faber Ltd

William Shakespeare, *As You Like It*, *Henry V*, *Macbeth*, *A Midsummer Night's Dream*, *The Winter's Tale* (all available in the Arden Shakespeare)

Sophocles, *Antigone*, translated by Marianne McDonald (Nick Hern Books, 2000)

Endnotes

1. Declan Donnellan, *The Actor and the Target* (Nick Hern Books, 2002, p. 30).

2. Sanford Meisner, *Sanford Meisner on Acting* (Vintage, 1987, p. 43).

3. *Ibid.* (p. 49).

4. Harold Guskin, *How to Stop Acting* (Methuen, 2004, p. 95).

5. Sir Richard Eyre, taken from email correspondence.

Other Books for Actors from NHB

ACTIONS
The Actors' Thesaurus
Marina Caldarone and Maggie Lloyd-Williams

THE ACTING BOOK
John Abbott

ACTING AND REACTING
Tools for the Modern Actor
Nick Moseley

THE ACTOR AND THE TARGET
Declan Donnellan

BEYOND STANISLAVSKY
The Psycho-Physical Approach to Actor Training
Bella Merlin

THE COMPLETE STANISLAVSKY TOOLKIT
Bella Merlin

FINDING YOUR VOICE
A Step-by-Step Guide for Actors
Barbara Houseman

THE GOLDEN RULES OF ACTING
Andy Nyman

HANDBOOK OF ACTING TECHNIQUES
Edited by Arthur Bartow

IMPROVISATION IN REHEARSAL
John Abbott

A SCREEN ACTING WORKSHOP
Mel Churcher

TACKLING TEXT [AND SUBTEXT]
A Step-by-Step Guide for Actors
Barbara Houseman